# he Definitive Guide

HARRY MAX

TAYLOR RAY

201 W. 103rd Street
Indianapolis, Indiana 46290

# Skype: The Definitive Guide

**This Book Is Safari Enabled**

 The Safari® Enabled icon on the cover of your favorite technology book means the book is available through Safari Bookshelf. When you buy this book, you get free access to the online edition for 45 days.

Safari Bookshelf is an electronic reference library that lets you easily search thousands of technical books, find code samples, download chapters, and access technical information whenever and wherever you need it.

To gain 45-day Safari Enabled access to this book:

- Go to http://www.quepublishing.com/safarienabled
- Complete the brief registration form
- Enter the coupon code A2KL-STGL-BGJP-5T1Q-6MB8

If you have difficulty registering on Safari Bookshelf or accessing the online edition, please e-mail customer-service@safaribooksonline.com.

Library of Congress Cataloging-in-Publication Data

Max, Harry.
  Skype : the definitive guide / Harry Max, Taylor Ray.
    p. cm.
  Includes bibliographical references and index.
  ISBN 0-321-40940-X (pbk. : alk. paper)
    1. Internet telephony.  2. Skype (Electronic resource)    I. Ray, Taylor.  II. Title.

TK5105.8865.M39 2006
621.3850285'4678--dc22                                      2006004240

07 06 05 6 5 4 3 2 1

Interpretation of the printing code: the rightmost double-digit number is the year of the book's printing; the rightmost single-digit number, the number of the book's printing. For example, a printing code of 05-1 shows that the first printing of the book occurred in 2005.

# Contents

## 4    Details of Using Skype
for the First Time  . . . . . . . . . . . . . . . . . . . **72**

# Foreword

When Janus and I started Skype in 2002, we were hoping to use peer-to-peer technology to generate a more customer-driven communication market. Our vision was to create a software application that would change how people communicate online and alter the economics of the telephony industry as a result. We wanted consumers to benefit directly from new products and services, and we wanted to accelerate the pace of innovation.

Today, our vision is a reality. Skype is the fastest growing Internet service in history, with over 75 million users worldwide, 10,000 affiliates, and an evolving community of hardware and software companies working to support a full Skype ecosystem. Our recent acquisition by eBay is another step along this path. We believe free voice is going to fundamentally change the nature of e-commerce, and over the next few years, our goal is to make Skype the world's largest online communication company.

My hope is that *Skype: The Definitive Guide* will help you better understand what Skype is and how you can get the most out of it.

*Niklas Zennström, CEO and cofounder, Skype*

# Preface

It's been many years since Brendan Kehoe wrote *Zen and the Art of the Internet* to demystify some of the key ideas behind "the Net," including how to use e-mail, share files, and create Web pages using HTML. When *Zen and the Art of the Internet* was published, Amazon.com was barely a year old. Can you imagine life without Amazon, Netflix, or Google?

More recently, the U.S. Supreme Court heard arguments about the legality of file sharing and whether it promotes innovation or invites theft from movie studios and record companies. Can you imagine modern music distribution without an MP3 player or iPod?

And indeed, this is where our story begins, because file sharing using advanced peer-to-peer networking technology is finally delivering on the promise of "communicating with other nations as if it were a commonplace occurrence." In the same way that the nature of e-mail transformed how we interact on a daily basis, Skype is now changing how and when we call one another, creating new habits of communication as a result.

Traditionally, the act of placing a telephone call required specialized equipment and a dedicated circuit-switched network that callers had to pay to use. Skype uses the Internet as the network, so callers make crystal-clear calls from computer to computer to anywhere in the world free of charge, or from computer to landline (or wireless) phone for a fraction of the cost. And in countries where the telephone infrastructure is outdated or not well developed, Skype makes the experience of calling to and from these places better. The process is reliable; the quality is better; and communicating is dramatically less expensive.

Skype is the fastest-growing communication service in the world, with more than 75 million registered users and more than 150,000 new users being added each day. Like the advent of e-mail, the Skype phenomenon is changing the way we communicate. It's changing how we organize communications and how we incorporate new technology into the patterns of our personal and professional lives.

Our hope is that this book will help you understand Skype and the basics of the technology. If you're not yet using Skype, this book provides easy-to-follow steps for installing and using it effectively. If you are already using Skype, this book shows you how other people are taking advantage of it and how to optimize your own use of Skype.

*Harry Max and Taylor Ray*
*Mountain View, California*
*skypeguide@metamax.com*

## Target Audience for This Book

This book is both for people who are new to Skype and for existing Skype users who want to optimize their use of Skype. This book is designed to get new users up and running quickly on Skype, and for existing Skype users, this book offers a comprehensive explanation of Skype's features and functions. For network administrators and IT personnel, this book covers Skype's architecture and security model, as well as advanced configuration topics.

## How This Book Is Organized

Chapters 1 and 2 present the essence of what you need to know to understand, install, configure, and use Skype using Microsoft Windows and Mac OS X. Chapters 3 and 4 provide in-depth installation and configuration procedures for beginning computer users and for users of the Pocket PC and Linux operating systems. Chapter 5 describes how to use all of Skype's features and functions. Chapter 6 describes how Skype is being used all over the world, and Chapter 7 outlines the steps to take when Skype is not working properly. Appendixes A, B, and C cover more technical topics: the Skype architecture, security model, and advanced configuration.

# Acknowledgments

We are indebted to the many people who made this book possible. First and foremost, we need to thank Dennis Allison for his prompting, guidance, encouragement, and support. We also wish to thank Howard Hartenbaum, without whose unwavering support this book simply would not have been published, and Niklas Zennström, who gave us the green light to move forward.

We thank Karen Gettman, executive editor at Addison-Wesley, for her flexibility, clear direction, and patience. We wish to thank the amazing Skype team, in particular Kurt Sauer, for his dedication and lucid explanations; David Rosnow, for answering questions at all hours; Henry Gomez, Kelly Larabee, Janus Friis, Stefan Oberg, and the awesome Skype developers, for creating such excellent software; and Pooj Preena, Bertrand Lathoud, and the rest of the Skype team, who made this book a priority.

We would also like to thank Sheri Cain, our developmental editor; Nikolai Lokteff, our illustrator; the supportive staff at Pearson Education; and our stellar reviewers, without whom this book would be quite unintelligible.

Special thanks also go to our friends, family members, and associates, who often endured "the book excuse" for many months on end. In particular, we want to thank James Taylor (the chemist, not the singer), Mother Sue, Papa Bruce, Lisa Taylor, Beth Ann and Susie Allen, Ann Swanberg, Judith Gable, Chris Miller, Jim LeBrecht, Michael Ehrenberg, David Bell, Todd Cotton, Richard Chuang, Mike Min, Ken Bielenberg, Mark Finnern, Jonathan Simonoff, Jeff Beale, Mark Interrante, Bo Holland, John Perry Barlow, the Information Architecture Institute board of directors, and Nick and his gang at Dana Street Coffee Roasting Company.

Last, we want to recognize Adobe Systems for supporting Adobe FrameMaker, the best professional word-processing software available, period.

# About the Authors

**Harry Max** is the CIO for Debix, Inc., a start-up focused on solutions for identity theft prevention. As an early Web pioneer, Harry designed the first secure online shopping cart (Virtual Vineyards/Wine.com) and founded Public Mind, a system for customer-driven innovation once used by Pyra Labs (acquired by Google), Handspring, Foveon, Kontiki (acquired by Verisign), the DMA, QuickArrow, and Skype. Max has worked with Apple Computer, Silicon Graphics, HP, O'Reilly and Associates, SAP, and DreamWorks Animation. He is also a development coach who works with creative technology professionals and is an active member of the Board of Advisers for the Information Architecture Institute.

**Taylor Ray** is an avid Skype user and former Deloitte & Touche consultant who now spends her time helping smart people become better understood. She has undergraduate degrees in linguistics and neuroscience and a graduate degree in adult education. She splits her time between Silicon Valley and Los Angeles, where she is pursuing a career in comedic film and television.

In this chapter,
you will learn:

What Skype is

·

Why Skype is an important new
tool for communicating

·

How Skype works at a basic level

·

Skype's major features
and functions

·

The origins of the Skype
technology

# What Is Skype?

## Skype Basics

Skype is the most popular Internet voice communication service in the world. More than 75 million people use Skype—more than all the other Internet voice providers combined.

Skype is simple to use. It lets you reach out across continents, borders, countries, and time zones to make crystal-clear voice calls, send instant messages, transfer digital files, and make video calls almost anywhere in the world for free. You can also call people on their ordinary phones and cell phones for a fraction of the cost of a traditional call.

Skype is changing the way people think about communications. Because the Skype communication signals are carried over the Internet, the major costs associated with traditional phone systems are eliminated. And because the phone company isn't controlling the amount of time you spend conversing, you can communicate for as long as you want.

Skype is also changing *how* people communicate. Because voice and IM are integrated into one application, you can quietly communicate back and forth with text and then switch seamlessly to voice when it's easier to talk than type. Skype also provides an important sense of "presence"—who is online and whether they are available—so you know ahead of time whether someone is willing and able to communicate.

People use Skype in a variety of ways:

- Family members on international business trips open Skype connections and leave them open so they can talk to loved ones back home any time of the day.

- Working parents use Skype to monitor activity at their homes.

- Small development groups hold long international conference calls while sending instant messages (IMs) and documents back and forth during the call.

- Travelers in hotels, on international flights, or on cruises (which offer Internet connectivity) make calls for a small fraction of the price of a long-distance call.

## A Global Application

Skype Technologies was the first company to deliver clear and consistent calls over the Internet, and as a result, Skype is used in almost every country in the world.

At present, the largest groups of Skype users reside in Europe, Asia, and North America. The fastest-growing group of Skype users is in Asia—in particular, China—as a result of the rapid adoption of broadband connectivity and the expense and poor quality associated with the traditional phone system.

## Brief Overview of Features

Skype is a full-featured and stable communication application. It has capabilities and graphical user interfaces for the following:

- Making person-to-person calls
- Making conference calls
- Making video calls
- Chatting (sending and receiving IMs)
- Transferring files
- Managing Skype accounts

With each update of the Skype application, convenient new features become available. For a list of the major features and capabilities currently available with Skype, see the tables later in this chapter.

# How Skype Is Unique

Skype is different from other Internet voice applications for these reasons:

**Free Skype to Skype**—Calls between Skype accounts are free of charge. Because Skype was designed and built completely independently of the traditional Public Switched Telephone Network (PSTN) infrastructure, Skype calls are routed completely over the Internet. Most other voice applications are hybrid solutions that work only in concert with the traditional phone system.

**Peer-to-peer (P2P) network**—Skype is built on a mature P2P networking technology that works virtually flawlessly, is adaptable to different network conditions, and is designed to expand without limits.

**Installation and configuration**—Installing and using Skype is straightforward. This is a major force driving adoption. Skype runs on most popular computing platforms and many communication devices.

**Works with firewalls**—Skype's unique P2P networking technology traverses the majority of firewalls and Network Address Translation (NAT) devices that are required for broadband connectivity. Skype is not limited by the Session Initiation Protocol (SIP) standard developed by the telecom companies.

**Broad adoption**—Skype has more than 75 million users. Increasingly, the people you are likely to call will be available through the Skype network.

**Sound quality**—Under most conditions, Skype has excellent sound quality, which can surpass the clarity of traditional phone, cellular, and non-Skype Internet calls.

**Security**—Calls, IMs, video calls, and file transfers are encrypted end-to-end using the Advanced Encryption Standard. It is impossible to intercept and eavesdrop on Skype-to-Skype communications.

**Growing ecosystem**—Companies such as Intel, Motorola, Siemens, Linksys, Kodak, Plantronics, Logitech, Boingo, and Sony are already producing products to work in concert with Skype. Plus Skype's open architecture and close relationship with its developer community support a thriving marketplace for third-party software applications. As more people use Skype, the larger the network becomes, and the greater the financial incentives for companies to build products to support and extend Skype's capabilities.

# Overview of How Skype Works

Skype takes advantage of advanced P2P networking technology to establish and route connections directly between computers, instead of forcing calls through a company's centralized servers. Unlike other voice service providers, the Skype P2P network grows more powerful with each new Skype user who comes online, continually improving the network's capacity to connect people.

Skype works on most popular operating systems (Windows 2000 and XP, Mac OS X, Linux, and personal digital assistants running Pocket PC), with the appropriate look and feel for each platform. Talking, sending IMs, and transferring files among different platforms are as seamless as sending and receiving e-mail across platforms.

Getting started with Skype is easy and straightforward. Regardless of the platform you use, you simply do the following:

1. Download and install Skype from the Skype Web site.

2. Register to create a Skype account.

3. Plug in a headset or phone that works with your computer (or use your built-in microphone and speakers).

4. Start using Skype.

In general, you don't need to know anything about computer networking, firewall and router configuration, or any other networking gear. Plus there is no need for a special service plan or any dedicated hardware.

Skype also works on many different devices: desktop computers, laptop computers, personal digital assistants (PDAs), residential cordless phones that support Skype, as well as a new breed of multimode cellular phones that support Wi-Fi connections to the Internet (see Figure 1-1).

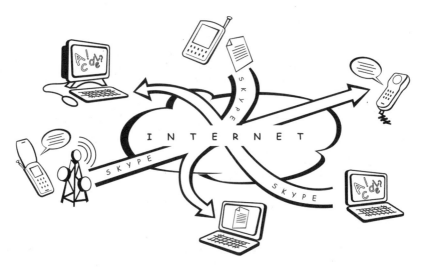

**Figure 1–1**   Skype works on a variety of devices

On a computer, Skype works like any software program that runs in the background when not being used and moves to the foreground when needed. In this way, Skype is similar to existing IM applications like ICQ, AOL Instant Messenger, and Yahoo! Instant Messenger, and to applications like GoogleTalk, Gizmo, Net2Phone, and MSN Messenger.

Skype works slightly differently depending on the device you're using, but the basic Skype-to-Skype calling operations are the same. You simply select someone from your Contacts List and click a button to make the call.

Skype offers various features that let you search for other Skype users, send IMs, transfer files, and manage calls. Skype also allows you to make and receive calls to people using traditional phones.

If you have access to the Internet, there is no charge for using Skype for voice or video calls, instant messaging, and transferring files between two Skype accounts (and for conference calls to as many as five Skype accounts). Calls from one Skype account to another are always free.

## SkypeOut

As mentioned in the preceding section, calls from one Skype account to another are free. But what if you want to use Skype to call someone on his traditional landline, business, or cell phone? When you want to use Skype to call someone who is using a traditional phone, Skype offers a fee-based service called SkypeOut.

With SkypeOut, you prepurchase minutes (similar to a calling card) to make calls that originate on the Skype network and terminate on the traditional telephone network. This allows you to call anyone, regardless of whether she has a Skype account, and it makes the payment process straightforward. When you call someone using SkypeOut, you simply use Skype to dial the phone number and connect. The person you are calling will be unaware that you are calling from Skype (see Figure 1-2).

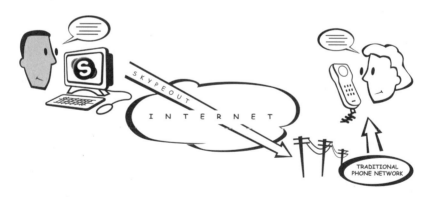

**Figure 1–2**   Calling out of the Skype network to a regular phone

SkypeOut is a fee-based feature because companies called *termination providers* charge money to provide a gateway to connect SkypeOut calls to traditional telephone networks. Skype Technologies purchases access to the gateway on behalf of Skype users and then sells this access as SkypeOut credit.

WARNING    Skype cannot be used for dialing emergency services anywhere in the world, such as 911 in the United States. If you try to call 911 using Skype, you will not be connected.

## SkypeOut Costs

SkypeOut offers two rate classes: SkypeOut Global Rates, which cover calls to the 25 most popular landline (and certain cellular) telephone destinations, and SkypeOut Individual Rates, which cover all other destinations.

### SkypeOut Global Rates

SkypeOut global rates are straight price-per-minute rates to 25 of the most popular landline (and certain cellular) telephone destinations. Currently, the rates work out to approximately 2 cents U.S. per minute.

Destinations include Argentina (Buenos Aires), Australia, Austria, Belgium, Canada (landline and cellular), Chile, China, Denmark, Estonia, France, Germany, Greece, Hong Kong (landline and cellular), Ireland, Italy, Mexico (Mexico City, Monterrey), the Netherlands, New Zealand, Norway, Poland, Portugal, Russia (Moscow, St. Petersburg), Singapore (landline and cellular), South Korea, Spain, Sweden, Switzerland, Taiwan, the United Kingdom, the United States (landline and cellular) except Alaska and Hawaii, and the Vatican. Skype is continually expanding its services, so check the Web site (www.skype.com) for the most current information.

SkypeOut charges are determined by the location of the gateway to the traditional telephone network, not the origin of the call. In other words, SkypeOut rates are calculated not by where you are calling from, but *where you are calling*. See Chapter 5 for more information.

### SkypeOut Individual Rates

SkypeOut individual rates are straight price-per-minute rates to landline or cellular telephone destinations in the remainder of the world.

Depending on where you are calling (and on whether you are calling a landline or cell phone), the individual rates currently range from 2 cents U.S. per minute to Australia to approximately $1.57 U.S. per minute to East Timor (the most expensive destination in the world to call).

SkypeOut credit must be purchased through the Skype Store (www.skype.com/store/). The rates are per minute, and calls are rounded up to the next minute.

NOTE    If your billing address is in the European Union, you will be charged a 15 percent Value Added Tax (VAT) when you buy SkypeOut credit. Your account will be credited, however, and your calls will be shown on your call list without the VAT.

Refer to the Skype Web site for the most current pricing and billing information. See Chapter 5 for information on how to purchase SkypeOut credit.

# SkypeIn

Once again, calls from one Skype account to another are always free. But what if someone using a landline or cell phone wants to call you on your computer, laptop, or PDA? For the times when people using traditional phones want to talk to you, Skype offers a fee-based service called SkypeIn.

With SkypeIn, you can buy one or more phone numbers that are associated with your Skype account. SkypeIn allows you to have local phone numbers in cities, states, and countries where you have friends, family members, or important customers who want to reach you regularly.

When you have SkypeIn and someone calls you from a landline or cell phone, he dials a regular phone number, hears a normal telephone "ring," and is unaware that the call is being received by a Skype user.

This means that you can give someone your number and she can call you anywhere in the world, regardless of whether you are at home using your computer or away from home using your laptop, Wi-Fi phone, or PDA running Pocket PC. No matter where you are, your Skype will ring. SkypeIn allows people to contact you with a phone number (that is local to them) without their knowing where you happen to be.

Here's an example: Let's say you live in Paris, and your brother lives in San Francisco. You can talk to him for free if both of you use your Skype accounts. Or you can purchase a SkypeIn number that is local to San Francisco, so your brother can dial this "local" phone number to talk with you in Paris, thus avoiding the long-distance charges (see Figure 1-3).

SkypeIn is a fee-based service because Skype Technologies purchases blocks of phone numbers from various phone companies to make them available to Skype users worldwide. There are also fees associated with the process of routing calls from the traditional phone system to the Internet, which Skype Technologies oversees and manages. Skype Technologies provides these numbers to Skype users, and manages the connection process and the billing associated with them.

**Figure 1-3**    Calling into a "local" number in a different
                  locale from Skype

NOTE    Existing telephone phone numbers currently cannot be transferred to a Skype account.

At the time of this printing, SkypeIn numbers were available in Denmark, Finland, France, Hong Kong SAR, China, Poland, Sweden, the United Kingdom, and many area codes in the United States. Skype is continually adding new countries and area codes. Currently, the rates work out to approximately $10 U.S. for a three-month subscription and $30 U.S. for an annual subscription. Please refer to the Skype Web site for the most current information.

NOTE    Skype includes free voicemail with a SkypeIn subscription.

# Devices That Work with Skype

Skype works with a variety of devices, such as headsets, microphones and speakers, USB handsets, Bluetooth wireless devices, and more.

## Desktop Computer

On your desktop computer, Skype works like any application program on Windows 2000 or XP, Mac OS X, or Linux. To use Skype, you need either an inexpensive headset or a microphone and speakers. Decent headsets can be acquired from the Skype Store or a retailer in the United States such as Radio Shack for as little as $12 U.S., and some people claim that the inexpensive headsets work as well as the more expensive ones on PCs. You *do not* have to have a fancy or expensive headset to enjoy using Skype.

Companies like Plantronics and Logitech sell premium headsets with features such as noise cancellation, higher-quality speakers, and folding capabilities in different styles at prices ranging from $12 to $75 U.S. Companies like Motorola sell wireless Bluetooth headsets for approximately $100 U.S.

You can also use a USB handset like the CyberPhone or the Linksys cordless VoIP phone. USB handsets plug into your computer's USB port, which you can use much like a traditional telephone. USB handsets cost approximately $75 U.S. Alternatively, you can use a residential dual-mode cordless phone, which rings in at around $175 U.S.

Webcams are available from companies such as Logitech, Creative Labs, and Hewlett-Packard. They range in price from $20 to $150 U.S., depending on image resolution and features like a built-in microphone and the ability to track facial movements.

## Wireless Laptops or PDAs Running Pocket PC

Skype is not restricted to desktop computers. Skype also runs on Internet-capable laptops and PDAs running Pocket PC over home wireless networks or Wi-Fi hotspots (or newly emerging Wi-MAX networks). Therefore, you can use Skype on a portable device at any hotspot.

Increasingly, hotspot providers are opening their paid wireless networks to Skype users. This gives Skype users good coverage and lets them access the Skype network to make calls for little to no cost. These Skype-friendly hotspot providers are motivated to do this in the hope that some of the Skype users will also pay for services such as Web access or broadband content. Did you know that if you're using Skype on a mobile device in London, you can use any one of Broadreach Networks's 350 hotspots to make calls?

Another popular way to use Skype is to access the Internet from a broadband cellular network data connection. Most cell phone companies offer digital data capabilities, which means you can access their networks either by connecting your laptop to your cell phone with a special cable or by using a cellular data PC card. A cellular data connection allows you to access the Internet using the cellular network so you can surf the Web, IM, send e-mail, and make Skype calls for the price of a data connection (see Figure 1-4).

## Residential Cordless and Dual-Mode Internet Phones

Residential cordless Internet phones are cordless phones with a base station that can be connected to a USB port on a computer instead of being connected to a traditional telephone socket. These residential cordless

Voice over Internet Protocol (VoIP) phones let you move the handset up to 150 feet away from your PC.

Residential cordless Internet phones, such as the Linksys cordless VoIP phone, display your Skype Contacts List so you can see who is online, allowing you to receive calls and to make Skype or SkypeOut calls at the touch of a button.

Residential dual-mode Internet phones, such as the Olympia cordless DUALphone, are cordless phones that can be connected to a traditional telephone socket *and* a USB port on your computer. Essentially, a dual-mode phone is an ordinary landline phone and Skype phone combined (see Figure 1-5).

**Figure 1–4**  Skype over a broadband cellular network

**Figure 1–5**  Using a Skype-enabled cordless home or office phone

Here's how to make a call using either a residential cordless phone or a dual-mode Internet phone:

- **Local calls**—Use Skype if the person you want to call has a Skype account. Or you can simply dial the phone number of the person you want to call. The call is routed from the handset to the base station, over the traditional phone network, to the person you are calling.

- **Long-distance calls**—Use Skype if the person you want to call has a Skype account. Or use SkypeOut to dial the phone number of the person you want to call. In this case, the call is routed from the handset to the base station, over the Internet, and through a gateway to the traditional phone network to the person you are calling.

## Multimode Cellular Phones

Multimode cellular phones are regular cell phones that can make calls over the cellular network(s) for which they were designed and over the Internet from a Wi-Fi connection or hotspot.

Essentially, a multimode cellular phone is a Skype-enabled Wi-Fi phone and an ordinary cell phone combined into one package. These multimode cellular phones allow you to make calls wherever and whenever you want, as long as you have a cell signal *or* a Wi-Fi connection to the Internet.

Multimode cellular phones display your Skype Contacts List when you have Wi-Fi access to the Internet so you can see who is online and make Skype or SkypeOut calls at the touch of a button.

To make a call with one of these phones, you can:

- **Use Skype** if you have Wi-Fi access to the Internet and the person you want to call has a Skype account.

- **Use SkypeOut** if you have Wi-Fi access to the Internet and the person you want to call either does not have a Skype account or can be reached only on a traditional phone.

- **Use the cellular network** and simply dial the phone number of the person you want to call.

The cost benefits of using Skype on a multimode cellular phone will depend on your cellular calling plan. If, for example, you have a national calling plan with free roaming, you may not gain much of a financial edge by using Skype to make a long-distance call within your country's national boundaries. You would save a lot of money by using SkypeOut when dialing an international number, however.

## Wi-Fi Phones

Wi-Fi phones are mobile handsets that can make calls over the Skype network from a Wi-Fi connection or hotspot. Although Wi-Fi phones are not as full featured as Skype on desktops, laptops, or PDAs running Pocket PC, they do allow you to access your Contacts List to see who is online and make Skype calls when you can connect to the Internet.

# Summary of Major Features

This section provides a list of the major features and functions of Skype. You should be aware that new features and capabilities become available with each update of the Skype application. Check the Skype Web site from time to time for information on the most current release of Skype.

NOTE    The features listed in the following tables do not necessarily map directly to Skype's user interface or menu options. They provide an outline of what you can do with the Skype application, however.

## Making Calls

Table 1-1 represents a summary of Skype's calling capabilities. For instructions on how to make calls, refer to Chapter 5.

**Table 1–1**   Features for Making Calls

| Function | Feature | Allows You To |
| --- | --- | --- |
| Making Calls | Call from Contacts | Select a Skype Name and start a call. |
| | Call from Dial Pad (SkypeOut) | Enter a number and start a call. |
| | Call from Received Calls | Select a received call and start a call. |
| | Search for Contacts | Search for Skype users on the global network using specific criteria. |
| | Display Contacts | See your personal list of contacts. |
| | Edit Profile | Change the profile information that other Skype users can see. |
| | Send a Contact | Send a Skype Name to another Skype user. |
| | Start a Conference Call | Select a group of contacts (or SkypeOut contacts) and start a conference call. |

*continues*

**Table 1–1**   Features for Making Calls *(continued)*

| Function | Feature | Allows You To |
|---|---|---|
| | Add Participants to a Conference Call | Add new people to an existing conference call. |
| | Start a Video Call | Select a Skype Name and start a video call. |
| | Start a Call within an IM Session | Click the Call button while chatting to start a call. |
| | View Call List | See a list of calls made and received, file transfers made and received, and voicemails received. |

## Receiving Calls

Table 1-2 represents a summary of Skype's support for receiving calls. For instructions on how to receive calls, refer to Chapter 5.

**Table 1–2**   Features for Receiving Calls

| Function | Feature | Allows You To |
|---|---|---|
| Receiving Calls | Accept or Reject a Call | Answer, ignore, or send a call to voicemail. |
| | View Profile of Caller | See the profile information of a caller. |
| | Accept or Reject an Authorization | Accept or reject a request from another Skype user to see your online status. |
| | Block Calls from Unknown Callers | Block calls from people you don't know. |
| | Block Calls from Known Callers | Block calls from people you know but don't want to talk to. |

## Voicemail

Table 1-3 represents a summary of Skype's voicemail capabilities. For instructions on how to use Skype voicemail, refer to Chapter 5.

**Table 1-3** Features for Configuring and Using Voicemail

| Function | Feature | Allows You To |
|---|---|---|
| Voicemail | Record a Personal Greeting | Record a greeting in your own voice. |
| | Voice Messaging | Leave a message for anyone in the Skype network without having to ring him or her. |
| | Retrieve Voicemails | Listen to your voicemails. |
| | Delete Voicemails | Remove voicemail messages from your computer. |

## Setting Preferences

Table 1-4 represents a summary of Skype's capabilities related to setting preferences. For instructions on how to set your Skype preferences, refer to Chapter 4.

**Table 1-4** Features Related to Setting Skype Preferences

| Function | Feature | Allows You To |
|---|---|---|
| Setting Preferences | Change Online Status | Set your availability indicator for others to see. |
| | Configure Privacy Settings | Specify who can and cannot contact you. |
| | Configure Basic and Advanced Skype Settings | Specify how you want Skype to function. |
| | Configure Notifications | Set the way you want to be notified of a call, IM, or file transfer. |
| | Configure Sound Alerts | Specify when you want to hear audio alerts. |
| | Configure Sound Devices | Set which sound devices you want Skype to use if needed. |
| | Configure Video | Enable video and specify video privacy settings. |
| | Create Hotkeys | Create shortcut keystrokes for basic Skype operations, if desired. |
| | Configure Voicemail | Specify how you want voicemail to function. |

## Instant Messaging or Chat

Table 1-5 represents a summary of Skype's IM capabilities. For instructions on how to use Skype IM, refer to Chapter 5.

**Table 1–5**  Features for Sending and Receiving IMs or Chat

| Function | Feature | Allows You To |
|---|---|---|
| Instant Messaging or Chat | Start a Chat Session | Send an IM to a Skype user. |
| | Start a Chat Session with a Group | Send an IM to a group of Skype users. |
| | Respond to an Instant Message | Receive an IM from another Skype user and reply to it. |
| | Set a Chat Topic | Name a chat with an individual or group of people. |
| | Bookmark a Chat | Keep a chat open and organized in a special place so you can correspond over long periods of time. |
| | View Chat History | See what has been written between you and a particular Skype user on a specific computer. |
| | Clear Chat History | Remove your chat history with a particular user from a specific computer. |

## Transferring Files

Table 1-6 represents a summary of Skype's file-transfer capabilities. For instructions on how to transfer files, refer to Chapter 5.

**Table 1–6**  Features for Transferring and Receiving Files

| Function | Feature | Allows You To |
|---|---|---|
| Transferring Files | Transfer a File to an Individual | Send a file to another Skype user. |
| | Transfer a File to a Group | Send a file to a group of Skype users simultaneously. |

*continues*

**Table 1–6**   Features for Transferring and Receiving Files *(continued)*

| Function | Feature | Allows You To |
|---|---|---|
| | Transfer Multiple Files to an Individual | Send multiple files to another Skype user. |
| | Transfer Multiple Files to a Group | Send multiple files to multiple Skype users. |
| | Drag and Drop Files to Contacts List | Click a file and drag the icon over a contact to send a file. |
| | Drag and Drop Files into a Chat Session | Click a file and drag the icon into an ongoing chat session to send a file. |
| | Block All File Transfers | Network administrators can configure Skype to block all file transfers in Microsoft Windows. |

# Profile and Account Management

Table 1-7 and Table 1-8 summarize Skype's capabilities related to managing your Skype profile and account. For details on how to update your profile, refer to Chapter 4. For instructions on how to manage your account, see Chapter 5.

**Table 1–7**   Features for Managing Your Skype Profile

| Function | Feature | Allows You To |
|---|---|---|
| Profile Management | Manage Public Profile Details | Add, change, or remove the profile information other Skype users can see. |
| | Manage Hidden Profile Details | Add or change e-mail addresses so others can find you. The e-mail addresses are kept private. |
| | Show Time | Display what time it is where you are. |
| | Show Number of Contacts | Display how many Skype contacts you have. |
| | Add a Picture to Your Profile | Upload any picture or graphic for other Skype users to see when they view your profile. |

*continues*

**Table 1–7** Features for Managing Your Skype Profile *(continued)*

| Function | Feature | Allows You To |
| --- | --- | --- |
| | Create Another Skype Account | Create additional Skype accounts with unique Skype Names for different purposes or personas. |
| | Import Contacts | Import existing contacts from existing contact management programs into Skype. |

**Table 1–8** Features for Managing Your Skype Account

| Function | Feature | Allows You To |
| --- | --- | --- |
| Account Management | Account Overview | See SkypeOut numbers called by month, a list of your Skype financial transactions, and your downloads; and purchase gift certificates. |
| | Account Settings | See the e-mail address you registered; and change your password, registered e-mail address, and displayed currency format. |
| | Call List | See SkypeOut numbers called by month. |
| | All My Purchases | Review a list of your Skype financial transactions. |
| | My Downloads | See any pictures, sounds, and other downloads. |
| | Gift Certificates | Learn about and purchase gift certificates. |
| | Purchase Skype Credit | Buy Skype credit so you can get Skype services and content, including SkypeOut so you can call regular telephone numbers using Skype. |
| | Purchase SkypeIn Subscription | Buy a number in a specific state or country so friends and colleagues can call you from a landline or cell phone. |
| | Redeem Vouchers | Use any vouchers you have received from Skype. |
| | Purchase Voicemail | Buy a voicemail subscription (if you don't have a SkypeIn number). |
| | View Account | See your purchase history and Skype account information. |

*continues*

**Table 1–8**   Features for Managing Your Skype Account *(continued)*

| Function | Feature | Allows You To |
|---|---|---|
| | Purchase Accessories | Buy a Skype starter kit, headsets, phones, and Webcams. |
| | Create Another Skype Account | Create additional Skype accounts with unique Skype Names for different purposes or personas. |
| | Personalize Skype | Buy sounds, ringtones, and pictures; and make WeeMees. |

# The Skype Story

The story of Skype is a modern tale of geography, luck, adventure, history, technology, and perseverance. It began in Copenhagen in 1997, when Niklas Zennström met Janus Friis.

At the time of their meeting, the Internet was still a relatively new consumer technology, but it was quickly gaining momentum as demand for Web sites and bandwidth was increasing worldwide. Internet service providers (ISPs) were proliferating, and computer-engineering graduates with business skills were in short supply.

Niklas was just such a graduate, having completed dual degrees in business and computer engineering from Uppsala University in Sweden. He was in Copenhagen building get2net, an ISP business for Tele2—a European independent phone company challenging the national telecom monopolies. Janus, ten years younger than Niklas, had no college degree and had been working as a tech-support representative at a competing ISP.

Niklas and Janus couldn't have been more different, but they met at Tele2 and connected immediately. Throughout that first year and into the next, they spent long hours dissecting Internet-related technology problems and brainstorming solutions. When Tele2 moved Niklas to Luxembourg and then to Amsterdam, Janus always followed to stay an integral part of the team.

## A Potential Solution

By 1999, the Internet gold rush was in full swing, but Niklas and Janus were still working inside a large company. They both felt as though they were missing out on the dot-com boom, and they wanted to strike out on their own. Janus persuaded Niklas to quit Tele2, and the two men evaluated new business ideas until a solid idea finally emerged—in the form of a potential solution to a bandwidth problem that Niklas experienced directly.

When Niklas was building get2net, he thought that it was absurd to have to buy bandwidth from companies in the United States to enable his European customers to watch movie trailers or listen to streaming music. The lack of a cost-effective way to transfer large files was a constant source of frustration.

Niklas and Janus thought they could solve this problem by storing files on subscribers' computers, allowing the computers to share information directly with one another (instead of routing traffic through traditional networking servers and other centralized equipment). Niklas and Janus also reasoned that they could provide subscribers access to these files through a special network browser that subscribers would pay to use.

## P2P Computing

Niklas and Janus's idea coincided with the hot topic of the day: P2P computing. Technically speaking, P2P computing is a way of allowing computers in a network to communicate directly with one another to exchange information or accomplish difficult tasks. Allowing computers to connect directly with one another prevents the network bottlenecks that result from using centralized equipment and mainframe computer servers.

P2P computing was emerging as the hot Internet technology, and it was being popularized by two entirely different P2P applications: ICQ and Napster.

ICQ, which stood for "I seek you," was the first fully functional instant-messaging application. ICQ allowed users to find one other; establish a P2P communication channel; and offered features such as presence, buddy lists, and "rapid messaging" with offline support. Napster, the MP3 music-sharing service, was experiencing a huge surge on college campuses worldwide, proving that P2P networks could be used to transfer large files effectively.

From a consumer-technology standpoint, ICQ and Napster were proving three things:

- ICQ was demonstrating that technology could be used to simplify the process of interconnecting users and allowing them to communicate efficiently on the Internet.

- Napster was demonstrating that P2P computing could be used to transfer large amounts of data.

- Both applications were demonstrating that ease of use and searchable directories were critical enablers for P2P networks.

With ICQ and Napster as evidence that P2P networks could solve some of the problems that Niklas had experienced at get2net, Niklas and Janus set out to build their own system.

## KaZaA

Niklas recruited four Estonian game programmers who had worked for him at Tele2. The system they built had a resilient software architecture that, among other things, made it impossible to shut down. It also included strong encryption and enabled users to see who in the network was online. Their new design became the next major innovation in consumer P2P networking technology.

In early 2001, Niklas and Janus formed a company called Consumer Empowerment to realize their vision of a consumer P2P network. They built a network browser called KaZaA to work in concert with their P2P network technology. They also licensed the use of their network to other companies.

In July 2001, Napster was shut down by the courts for reasons related to copyright infringement. Napster had generated a huge demand for this new form of music distribution, but there was no longer a way to satisfy it. Word of an alternative called KaZaA spread quickly.

The KaZaA network browser application was easy to use and worked well on top of the new P2P network technology. It allowed users to organize, view, and play media files through an integrated media jukebox. It supported file formats other than MP3. And unlike Napster, it had software and video clips. It also had patches for games and programs that were difficult to get from "official" Web sites because the developers' sites were too slow.

KaZaA became the application of choice for moving large electronic files, and the use of KaZaA skyrocketed. As traffic and downloading surged to tens of millions of users, the development team reinforced the network architecture, added new features and capabilities, and optimized the system as it scaled globally in real time.

Then, in January 2002, as the Dutch courts were deliberating the merits of a lawsuit against rights-management agency Buma/Stemra, KaZaA was sold to the Australian company Sharman Networks for an undisclosed sum.

## A New Idea

Niklas and Janus took some time off and then began to look for places where they could use their experience. They looked specifically at industries that relied on an inefficient centralized infrastructure and ones in which consumers could reap the benefits of the technology.

Telecommunications quickly became a candidate. Aside from historically delivering questionable "customer service," telecommunications relies on a heavy centralized infrastructure with many different types of networks that are expensive to build and maintain. Developing new services is difficult and takes a long time because these networks don't interoperate neatly. Moreover, real estate, buildings, and vast amounts of capital-intensive equipment (such as large mainframe computer servers, switches, lines, poles, and trucks) are required to run the business, contributing to large inefficiencies that translate into expensive services for consumers.

As Niklas and Janus were privately honing in on the decision to build a voice application, Niklas was approached by a partner representing Draper Investment Company, a boutique international venture capital firm with close ties to Silicon Valley. Together with Janus and close associate Geoffrey Prentice, the four hammered out a business plan, and Draper Investment Company provided the seed funding.

Skype was born.

The team decided to focus on building an application to deliver free voice calls computer to computer, with the assumption that if they could get massive adoption, they could provide value-added services and ultimately establish a complete telecommunications solution.

A voice application presented a special challenge, however, because for a voice application to succeed, there have to be enough people on the network who know one another and want to talk to one another. In addition, ease of use, connection stability, and call quality have to be as good as or better than what people have become accustomed to with landline and cell phones.

## Skype Beta

Niklas and Janus hired the Estonian programmers again, this time to build a software application that would go beyond KaZaA's architecture, work behind firewalls and Network Address Translation (NAT) devices, install and configure easily, and be simple and straightforward to use.

The team spent a year developing the system and quietly launched Skype beta in August 2003, with the hopes that the application would ''go viral''—that people would get their friends and family members to use Skype, and that they in turn would get *their* friends and family members to use Skype.

Six months later, more than 6 million copies of the software had been downloaded worldwide, and in February 2004, Niklas and Janus were featured on the cover of *Fortune* magazine. A little over a year later, Skype passed its 100 million downloads mark.

## Skype Today

Today, Skype has more than 75 million members and is being used in more than 225 countries and territories in 27 languages throughout the world. Skype users can now call into and out of the traditional phone system, as well as use Skype for conference calls, IMs, file transfers, and video calls.

Worldwide, Skype serves more voice minutes than all the other Internet voice communication service providers combined.

In addition, there is an extensive and growing list of partnerships with hardware, software, ISP, and media companies that are developing products and services that complement Skype.

On September 12, 2005, eBay agreed to acquire Skype Technologies SA for approximately $2.6 billion in cash and stock. Said Janus, "Together, we feel we can really change the way that people communicate, shop, and do business online."

In this chapter,
you learn how to:

Download and install Skype

•

Verify the equipment you need

•

Create a Skype account

•

Set your initial preferences

•

Use Skype for the first time to
make a call, send an instant
message (IM), and transfer a file

# Skype Quick Start

Downloading and installing Skype can be done successfully without instructions, but a summary of the process is included in this chapter to help you get you up and running quickly on Skype.

This chapter is for computer-savvy users who don't need detailed instructions. It summarizes Chapters 3 and 4, and covers installation procedures for Microsoft Windows and Mac OS X. For instructions on other operating systems (Linux and Pocket PC), please see Chapter 3.

If you are a beginning computer user, someone who wants more detailed downloading and installing instructions, or someone who wants to install Skype on Linux or Pocket PC, please refer first to Chapter 3 and then to Chapter 4.

To install and run Skype, you generally don't need to know anything about networking, firewalls, routers, or other networking gear. You should be aware, however, that if you have a software firewall installed, you may have to reconfigure it to work with Skype. This is covered in Appendix C.

## Process Overview

Here is a brief overview of the process of getting started:

1. Download and install the appropriate Skype application program from the Skype Web site (www.skype.com).

2. Register and create a Skype account.

3. Plug in a headset, microphone and speakers, or phone that works with your computer.

4. Test that your setup is working properly.

5. Start making calls, sending IMs, or transferring files to your friends, family members, and business associates.

# Equipment and Requirements

To get the best sound quality and to be able to take advantage of the advanced features in Skype, you need a reasonably fast computer, a headset or a set of speakers and a microphone, and a broadband connection (DSL, cable, or high-speed cellular wireless). For best performance, your computer should have approximately the capabilities shown in Table 2-1.

**Table 2–1**   Recommended Configuration

|  | Operating System | Processor, RAM, and Hard Disk Space | Other |
|---|---|---|---|
| Windows PC | Windows 2000 or XP | 1GHz<br><br>512MB RAM<br><br>30MB free on hard disk | Full-duplex sound card (1998 or newer). Headset or speakers and microphone.<br><br>USB handset is optional. |
| Macintosh | Mac OS X 10.3 or newer | 1.25GHz G3, G4, or G5<br><br>512MB RAM<br><br>30MB free on hard disk | USB headset. Headset or speakers and microphone.<br><br>VoIP phone is optional. |

# Download and Install Skype

To install Skype on your computer, simply download the Skype application from the Skype Web site, and follow the instructions in the installation wizard.

Here are the steps for downloading and installing Skype on Microsoft Windows and Mac OS X. For detailed instructions and directions for installing in other operating systems, see Chapter 3.

1. Point your Web browser to www.skype.com to get the latest version of Skype.

1. Select the download menu, and click the icon appropriate for your operating system.

2. Save the installation file.

   • Microsoft Windows users: Save the installation file (Skype-Setup.exe) to your computer, and double-click the file to start installing Skype.

   • Mac OS X users: Double-click the Skype disk image mounted on your Desktop, and drag the Skype application to your Applications folder.

3. Launch Skype, and follow the Skype setup wizard.

4. Select a language, read the Skype license agreement, and accept the terms of the agreement.

5. Select **Launch Skype** to create a new Skype account.

# Create a New Skype Account

When you have completed downloading and installing Skype, you need to create a new account to register as a Skype user.

## Microsoft Windows Users

When the Skype Setup Wizard is complete, the Sign In window is displayed. Because you don't yet have a Skype account, you will need to create one.

To create a new Skype account, follow these steps:

1. Click the **Don't Have a Skype Name?** link in the Sign In window. The Create Account window is displayed, as shown in Figure 2-1.

**Figure 2–1**   Create Account window

2. Choose a Skype Name and password.

3. Enter a valid e-mail address that will be used to create your Skype account and to communicate with you about lost password information.

NOTE    If you do not enter a valid e-mail address and you lose your password, there will be no way to recover it, and you will have to abandon your Skype account and create a new one.

4. Read and accept the Skype licensing agreement.

5. Fill out some basic information for your Personal Profile, which is how other Skype users will be able to find you.

   The information you enter may be displayed for others to see, *with the exception of your e-mail address*. Personal Profile information is not required for you to use Skype, and you can always change it later.

6. Be sure you are connected to the Internet.

7. Skype will try to log in to validate that you have chosen a unique Skype Name.

   Skype will notify you if you need to choose another Skype Name; otherwise, you will see the Skype main window.

The Skype user interface, or main window, is organized around a main area with three tabs (see Figure 2-2):

- **Contacts** displays the Skype Names of the people in your Contacts list and each person's online status. To call someone, select a Skype Name, and click the big green **Call** button. Alternatively, right-click a Skype Name, and select **Call** from the context menu to make a call.

- **Dial** displays a keypad where you can dial a number directly when calling outside the Skype network.

- **History** shows a list of recent calls, chats, and file transfers you've made, as well as the dates and times of these communications. It also shows where you saved files that were transferred to your computer. To call someone, select a Skype Name, and click the big green **Call** button. Alternatively, right-click a Skype Name, and select **Call** from the context menu to make a call.

The top of the Skype main window also includes a series of action buttons; an events area, where you can see missed calls and received voicemails; and a services section, where you can get information about your Skype account.

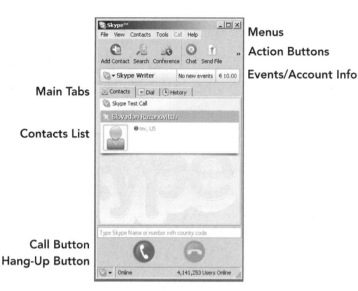

**Figure 2–2** Skype main window (Windows version)

The Skype application works in a standard way across a variety of functions. Typically, you *select* one or more Skype Names and then *do* something (call, send an IM, start a conference call, or transfer a file).

## Mac OS X Users

When you open Skype, you will see the Skype Sign-In window. Because you don't yet have a Skype account, you will need to create one. To create a new Skype account, follow these steps:

1. Click **Create a New Account**.

2. Choose a Skype Name and password.

3. Enter a valid e-mail address so you can recover your password if you forget it.

NOTE     If you do not enter a valid e-mail address and you lose your password, there will be no way to recover it, and you will have to abandon your Skype account and create a new one.

4. Read and accept the Skype licensing agreement.

5. Check **Remember My Name and Password on This Computer**; decide whether to launch Skype automatically when you log into OS X. Click **Create**.

   If your computer generally is not connected to the Internet, you should not select this option. You can change this setting later.

6. Be sure you are connected to the Internet.

   Skype will try to log in to validate that you have chosen a unique Skype Name.

   Skype will notify you if you need to choose another Skype Name; otherwise, you will see the Edit Profile window.

7. Fill out some basic information for your Personal Profile, which is how other Skype users will be able to find you.

   The information you enter may be displayed for others to see, *with the exception of your e-mail address.* The e-mail address in your Personal Profile may help other Skype users find you on the net-work (if they know your address). Your e-mail addresses are always kept private. Personal Profile information is not required for you to use Skype, and you can always change it later.

8. Click **Apply**. You will see the Skype main window.

The Skype user interface, or main window, is organized around a main area with three subsections (see Figure 2-3):

- **Contacts** displays the Skype Names of the people in your Contacts list and each person's online status. To call someone, select a Skype Name, and click the big green **Call** button. Alternatively, Control-click a Skype Name, and select **Call** from the context menu to make a call.

- **Dial** displays a keypad where you can dial a number directly when calling outside the Skype network.

- **Call List** shows a list of recent calls, chats, and file transfers you've made, as well as the dates and times of these communications. It also shows where you saved files that were transferred to your computer. To call someone, select a Skype Name, and click the big green **Call** button. Alternatively, Control-click a Skype Name, and select **Call** from the context menu to make a call.

The bottom of the Skype main window also includes two event bars and a text box for entering telephone numbers and Skype Names.

The Skype application works in a standard way across a variety of functions. Typically, you *select* one or more Skype Names and then *do* something (call, send an IM, start a conference call, or transfer a file).

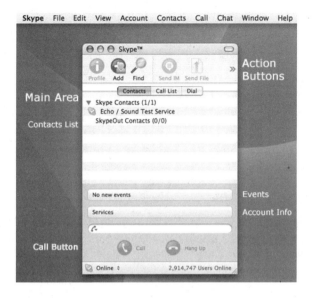

**Figure 2–3**   Skype main window (Mac OS X version)

# Make a Test Call

Before you start adding Skype Names, you may want to make a test call to ensure that your headset (or microphone and speakers) works properly. Be sure these devices are plugged in before you start.

Here is how to make a test call:

1. Select **Skype Test Call** in your Contacts list (or enter **echo123** in the text box at the bottom of the Skype main window), and click the big green **Call** button.

2. If your microphone and speakers (or headset) are working properly, you should hear a prerecorded voice asking you to leave a 10-second message that will then be played back to you.

3. Record your message.

4. If you hear the prerecorded message plus your own voice, you can safely assume that Skype is working properly.

5. If you hear the recording but don't hear your own voice in the playback, you will need to adjust your recording settings for your microphone.

6. To adjust the volume of your microphone, speakers, or headset, choose Start > Settings > Control Panel > Sounds and Audio Devices (Mac OS X users: Choose Apple > System Preferences > Sound).

## Microsoft Windows Users

To adjust your microphone settings, follow these steps:

1. On your computer, select Accessories > Entertainment > Sound Recorder.

2. Try to record your speech and play it back.

3. If you still can't hear your recording, go the Sounds and Audio section of Control Panel and try adjusting the microphone settings until the recording test works, or refer to Chapter 7 for more information.

4. To adjust the volume of your speakers or headset, go to the Sound Control Panel.

## Mac OS X Users

To adjust your microphone settings, follow these steps:

1. Open your System Preferences, select Sound, choose Input, and adjust the input level so that it registers your voice at approximately 75 percent.

2. If you still can't hear your recording, choose **Skype** > **Preferences Audio** to make sure that the audio input is set to use the appropriate audio input device.

   If that doesn't work, refer to Chapter 7 for more information.

3. To adjust the volume of your speakers or headset, use your keyboard audio control, or go to the Sound System Preference and increase the output volume.

NOTE    You can make a test call at any time by calling the Skype Name **echo123** answering service.

# Set Your Preferences

It's a good idea to set your preferences before you start making calls. You can set your preferences for a variety of configuration options, including general operations, privacy, notifications, sound alerts, sound devices, hotkeys, connection options, and voicemail. You can change your preferences anytime.

For a complete summary of preferences settings, see the "Preferences Menu Summary" section for your operating system in Chapter 4.

## Microsoft Windows Users

Here is how to set your preferences:

1. In the Skype main window, choose **Tools** > **Options** (see Figure 2-4).

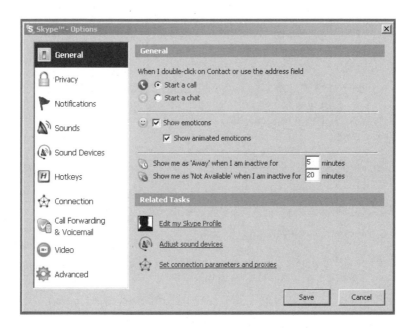

**Figure 2–4** Options console/General options

Note To exit any Options window, click **Cancel**. To save changes in any Options window, click **Save**. The changes will be adopted immediately. If you make a mistake, simply select the menu in the Options console, change the settings again, and click **Save** in the Options window.

2. Select the **General** menu at the top of the Options console (if it is not already selected).

3. Decide whether you want Skype to start a call or start a chat (IM session) when you double-click a contact; set your preferences for 'Away' and 'Not Available'; and click **Save** to save your changes.

   The double-click preference is a personal choice, and it depends on how you prefer to use Skype. Whereas many Skype users prefer to set this option to start a "conversation" by chatting (instant messaging), others prefer to start talking immediately.

   'Away' and 'Not Available' represent users' online status. Skype displays icons showing your online status so that other Skype users can know whether you are online and whether they can contact you.

4. Select the **Privacy** menu.

5. Decide whom you want to be allowed to call and chat with you, and click **Save** to save your changes.

   When you are first using Skype, you may want to allow anyone to call or chat. You can change these preferences at any time. If you are sure that you do not want people you may not know contacting you, opt to allow only the people from your Contacts list or only those you have authorized.

6. Select the **Notifications** menu.

7. Specify when you want be notified of an event with a small pop-up menu, and click **Save** to save your changes.

8. Select the **Sound Alerts** menu.

9. Specify when you want to be alerted of an event with a sound, and click **Save** to save your changes.

   To hear the default sound, click the left green **Play** button.

   To upload a sound file of your own or create your own ringtone, click the middle folder icon, select a .wav file from your collection, and click **Open**. To reset the sound to the Skype default, click the right red round **arrow button**.

10. Select the **Sound Devices** menu.

11. Select **Ring PC Speaker** to have Skype ring your speakers even if you have a headset plugged in, and click **Save** to save your changes.

12. Repeat these instructions for any of the other types of preferences you want to set.

NOTE    Because Skype users who have purchased voicemail can leave voicemail messages (even if you have not purchased a subscription to voicemail), you should record a personal greeting using the **Voicemail** menu.

## Mac OS X Users

Here is how to set your preferences:

1. Choose **Skype** > **Preferences**.

   The General window appears (see Figure 2-5).

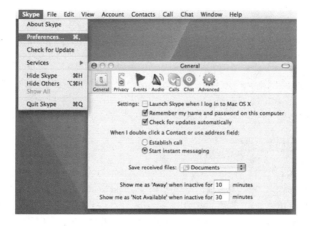

**Figure 2–5**  Preferences General window

2. Select the **General** icon (if it is not already selected).

3. Decide whether you want Skype to establish a call or start an IM when you double-click a contact, and set your preferences for 'Away' and 'Not Available.'

   The double-click preference is a personal choice, and it depends on how you like to begin communicating with people. Whereas many Skype users prefer to set this option to start a "conversation" by chatting (instant messaging), others want to start talking immediately.

   'Away' and 'Not Available' are online statuses. Skype displays icons showing your online status so that other Skype users can know whether you are online and whether they can contact you.

4. Select the **Privacy** icon.

5. Specify whom you want to be allowed to call and IM you.

   When you are first using Skype, you may want to allow anyone to call or IM. You can change any preferences at any time. If you are sure that you do not want people you may not know contacting you, opt to allow only the people from your Contacts list or only those you have authorized.

6. Select the **Events** icon.

   Make sure that the **Bounce Icon in the Dock** checkbox is checked.

7. Select the **Calls** icon.

8. Record a welcome message, because other Skype users who have voicemail can leave you a voicemail message (even if you don't have voicemail).

9. Repeat these instructions for any of the other types of preferences you want to set.

# Add Contacts

*Contacts* are people in the Skype network with whom you want to communicate. Your Contacts list will be empty when you first start Skype, so you will want to add contacts to make a call, send an IM, or transfer a file.

   You can add contacts in two ways: You can search the Skype network and add Skype Names from the search results, or you can let Skype scan your computer and automatically import contacts from an address book.

## Microsoft Windows Users

To add contacts by searching the Skype network, follow these steps:

1. Click the **Add Contact or Search** icon (see Figure 2-6).

2. Enter the name of the person you want to add to your Contacts list, and click **Search**.

   Skype will search the network and display a list of matches. If multiple matches are displayed, select a contact, and click the **Profile** icon in the search-results box to determine whether this is the person you want to add.

3. To add a contact to your Contacts list, make sure the correct contact is selected; then click the **Add Selected Contact** icon in the search-results box.

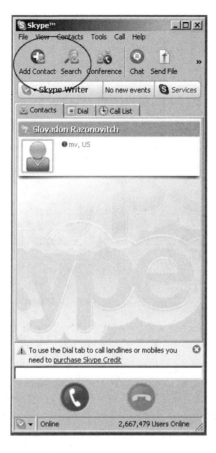

**Figure 2–6** Search the Skype network (for Windows)

4. Complete an authorization.

   When you add a new contact, Skype will ask you whether you want to allow or authorize this contact to see your contact details and online status. This is purely a personal preference.

   Authorizations are designed as part of Skype's privacy configurations. You can set your Skype preferences to allow calls from anyone, only from people in your Contacts list, or only from people you have authorized to see your contact details.

5. Type a message (optional).

6. Select an option to allow or disallow the contact to see when you are online, and click **OK** (see Figure 2-7).

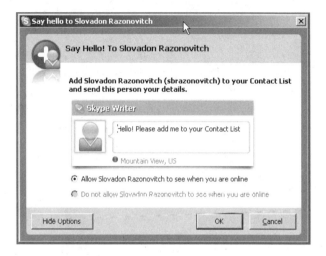

**Figure 2–7** Authorization (for Windows)

NOTE     When you have authorized someone to see your online status, you cannot revoke the authorization. You can block a user from contacting you, however. Blocking a user also prevents him from seeing your online status. See Chapter 5 for more information.

## Mac OS X Users

To add contacts by searching the Skype network, follow these steps:

1. Click **Find**, or choose **Contacts > Search for People**.

2. Enter the name of the person you want to add to your Contacts list, and click **Find**.

   Skype will search the network and display a list of matches, as shown in Figure 2-8. If multiple matches are displayed, you can select a contact and click the **Profile** icon in the search-results box to determine whether this is the person you want to add.

3. To add a contact to your Contacts list, make sure the correct contact is selected; then click the **Add** icon.

4. Complete an authorization request.

   When you add a new contact, you will be asked to complete an authorization request. This allows you to make a request to the person you are adding to "authorize" you to see when she is online. This also allows you to specify whether you want your new contact to see your online status.

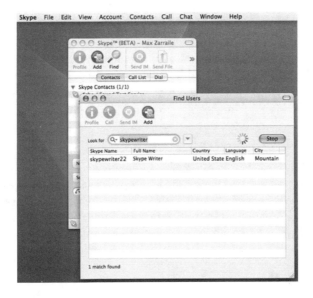

**Figure 2–8**  Search the Skype network (for Mac)

Authorizations are designed as part of Skype's privacy configurations. You can set your Skype preferences to allow calls from anyone, only from people in your Contacts list, or only from people you have authorized.

5. Type a message (optional).

6. Select an option to allow or disallow the contact to see when you are online, and click **OK** (see Figure 2-9).

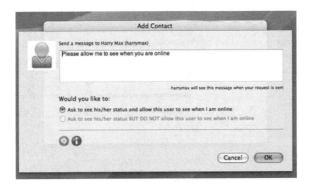

**Figure 2–9**  Authorization (for Mac)

When the contact has been added, you can call the contact, send an IM, or add more contacts.

NOTE     When you have authorized someone to see your online status, you cannot revoke the authorization. You can block a user from contacting you, however. Blocking a user also prevents him from seeing your online status. See Chapter 5 for more information.

## Import Contacts

You can let Skype scan for contacts automatically in an address book on your computer, including Microsoft Outlook, Outlook Express, Opera, MSN Messenger/Windows Messenger, Entourage, or the Apple Address Book.

To import contacts, choose **Contacts** > **Import Contacts**, and follow the import wizard. See Chapter 5 for more information.

# Make a Call

There are four ways to make a call using Skype:

- Select a Skype Name to highlight it, and click the big green **Call** button to initiate a call.

  This assumes that you have already added the name of the person to your Skype Contacts list or have identified the contact using Search.

- Double-click a Skype Name in the Skype Contacts list.

  This assumes that you have already added the name of the person you wish to call to your Skype Contacts list. If your Skype preferences are set to initiate a call when you double-click, the call will be initiated. Otherwise, a chat window will open, and you need to click the big green **Call** button. To change your preferences, see "Set Your Preferences" earlier in this chapter.

- Right-click a Skype Name, and select **Call** from the context menu. (Mac users: Control-click a Skype Name and select **Call** from the context menu.)

  This assumes that you have already added the name of the person to your Skype Contacts list or have identified the contact using Search.

- Type a Skype Name or conventional phone number, and click the big green **Call** button.

  You can make calls to traditional phone numbers if you have purchased SkypeOut credit. For more information, see the following section.

# Make a Call to a Landline or Cell Phone (SkypeOut)

Skype-to-Skype calls are always free. To call someone outside the Skype network, you need to buy SkypeOut credit for your account. To get access to your account page, go to the Skype Web site. You can also get to your account page from Skype by choosing **Tools** > **SkypeOut**. (Mac users: Choose **Account** > **SkypeOut**.)

To buy SkypeOut credit, follow these steps:

1. Log into your account, using your Skype Name and password.

2. Select **SkypeOut**.

3. Select the amount of credit you want to purchase, and select the payment method you want to use.

4. Switch back to Skype, enter a phone number in the format required by Skype, click the big green **Call** button, and start talking.

That's all there is to it.

NOTE    SkypeOut numbers must be entered in the international format using a plus sign +, country code, area code, and number. A valid number in the United States, for example, would be +14085551212 (the country code is 1; the area code is 408; and the number is 5551212).

# Start a Chat (Send an Instant Message)

The procedure for starting a chat (sending an IM) is similar to making a call. There are three ways to start a chat:

- Select a Skype Name in your Contacts list, and click the **Chat** icon in the Skype main window. (Mac users: Select a Skype Name, and click the **Send IM** icon.)

- Right-click a Skype Name, and select **Start Chat** from the context menu. (Mac users: Control-click a Skype Name, and select **Send Instant Message** from the context menu.)

- Double-click a Skype Name in your Contacts list (if you have configured Skype to start an IM versus a call). To do this, set your General preferences as described in "Set Your Preferences" earlier in this chapter.

You can start a multiperson chat by selecting multiple Skype Names in the Contacts list while holding down the Ctrl key and then clicking the

**Chat** icon. (Mac users: Select multiple Skype Names while holding down the Command key and then click the **Send IM** icon.)

# Transfer a File

The procedure for sending a file is similar to that for making a call or sending an IM. You can send files only to people who have authorized you, and the recipient of the file transfer must be online to accept the transfer before it can go through.

There are three ways to transfer a file:

- Select a Skype Name in your Contacts list, and click the **Send File** icon in the Skype main window.

- Right-click a Skype Name, and select **Send File** from the context menu. (Mac users: Control-click a Skype Name, and select **Send File**.)

- Alternatively, you can drag and drop a file into an open chat session.

NOTE   Skype allows system administrators to disable the file transfer capability. If the Skype application user interface for transferring files is grayed out, it means that someone has configured your Skype application to prevent you from sending or receiving files in this fashion. Refer to Appendix B or consult your system administrator for clarification or help.

# Update Your Personal Profile

Your Personal Profile contains information that allows other users to find your Skype Name on the Skype network. When you add information to your profile, you are making it available to anyone who has permission to see it—with the exception of your e-mail address. Your e-mail address is always kept private, but Skype users who know your e-mail address can use it to search for your Skype Name.

To add, change, or delete details in your profile, choose **File** > **Edit My Profile**. (Mac users: Choose **Account** > **My Profile**.) You also have the option of selecting a photo or uploading a bitmap or .JPEG file from your files. This picture is what callers will see when they Skype you and when they view your Skype Profile.

IN THIS CHAPTER,
YOU LEARN HOW TO:

DOWNLOAD SKYPE

•

INSTALL SKYPE IN WINDOWS 2000
AND XP, MAC OS X, LINUX, AND
POCKET PC

•

INSTALL THE SKYPE WEB TOOLBAR

•

UNINSTALL SKYPE

# Details of Installing Skype

This chapter is designed for beginning computer users and for people who want detailed instructions for downloading and installing Skype. This chapter includes some of the material covered in Chapter 2, but it provides a more detailed set of step-by-step procedures for downloading Skype from the Internet and installing it on a computer.

## Installation Summary

Downloading and installing Skype is simple and straightforward, provided that you have a stable connection to the Internet and meet the minimum system requirements listed in Table 3-1.

Here is a brief overview of the process of getting started, regardless of the computing platform you are using:

1. Download the appropriate Skype application program from the Skype Web site (www.skype.com).

2. Register and create a Skype account.

3. Plug in a headset, microphone and speakers, or phone that works with your computer.

4. Test that your setup is working properly.

5. Start making calls; sending instant messages (IMs); or transferring files to your friends, family members, or business associates.

Generally, you don't need to know anything about computer networking, firewall and router configuration, or other networking gear. Occasionally, however, a new Skype user may have trouble connecting to Skype for the first time because he has a software firewall installed.

If you have a software firewall such as Norton Personal Firewall, Trend Micro PC-cillin Internet Security, Zone Alarm Pro, McAfee Firewall Pro, or the one that comes with Windows XP Service Pack 2, in some cases you may need to reconfigure it to work with Skype. This and other advanced setup topics are covered in Appendix C.

To use Skype, you will *not* need a special voice service plan or special hardware (such as the type of telephony adapter that many voice application service providers require to translate the electrical signals in your phone into network information packets suitable for communicating over the Internet). You will need a headset, speakers and a microphone, or a USB handset.

# Things You Need to Know

To get the best sound quality and take advantage of the advanced features in Skype, you need a reasonably fast computer, a way to hear and speak (headset, handset, or set of speakers and a microphone), and a broadband connection to the Internet (DSL, cable, or broadband cellular wireless). You can install and use Skype with a dial-up connection over the traditional telephone network, however, as long as you are not uploading or downloading other data at the same time.

Headsets, microphones/speakers, and USB handsets are available at computer retailers; most office-supply stores; and many online retailers, including the Skype Accessories Store (www.skype.com/store/).

And although you don't need an expensive headset to get good sound quality, getting one with a built-in microphone will make a big difference in your Skype experience. Some people claim that the inexpensive headsets work as well as the more expensive ones on PCs.

## Minimum System Requirements

For you to be able to use Skype software after you install it, your computer must meet the minimum system requirements shown in Table 3-1.

**Table 3–1**   Minimum System Requirements

| | Operating System | Processor, RAM, and Hard Disk Space | Other |
|---|---|---|---|
| Windows PC | Windows 2000 or XP | 400MHz<br><br>256MB RAM<br><br>17MB free on hard disk | Full-duplex sound card (1998 or newer). Headset or speakers and microphone.<br><br>USB handset is optional. |

*(continues)*

**Table 3–1**   Minimum System Requirements *(continued)*

|  | Operating System | Processor, RAM, and Hard Disk Space | Other |
|---|---|---|---|
| Macintosh | Mac OS X 10.3 or newer | 667MHz G3, G4, or G5<br><br>256MB RAM<br><br>20MB free on hard disk | Headset or speakers and microphone.<br><br>USB handset is optional. |
| Linux | SuSE or newer, Mandrake 10.1 or newer, Fedora Core 3, Debian | 400MHz<br><br>256MB RAM<br><br>10MB free on hard disk | Full-duplex sound card (1998 or newer). Headset or speakers and microphone.<br><br>USB handset is optional. |
| Pocket PC | Windows Mobile 2003 for Pocket PC | 400MHz<br><br>Wi-Fi–enabled | Active Sync must be installed on your PC before you install Skype. |

## Recommended System Requirements

For you to take full advantage of Skype software after you install it, your computer should meet approximately the recommended system requirements shown in Table 3-2.

**Table 3–2**   Recommended System Requirements

|  | Operating System | Processor, RAM, and Hard Disk Space | Other |
|---|---|---|---|
| Windows PC | Windows 2000 or XP | 1GHz<br><br>512MB RAM<br><br>30MB free on hard disk | Full-duplex sound card (1998 or newer). Headset or speakers and microphone.<br><br>USB handset is optional. |
| Macintosh | Mac OS X 10.3 or newer | 1.25GHz G3, G4, or G5<br><br>512MB RAM<br><br>30MB free on hard disk | USB headset.<br><br>USB handset is optional. |

*(continues)*

**Table 3–2** Recommended System Requirements *(continued)*

|  | Operating System | Processor, RAM, and Hard Disk Space | Other |
|---|---|---|---|
| Linux | SuSE or newer, Mandrake 10.1 or newer, Fedora Core 3, Debian | 1GHz<br><br>512MB RAM<br><br>20MB free on hard disk | Full-duplex sound card (1998 or newer). Headset or speakers and microphone.<br><br>USB handset is optional. |
| Pocket PC | Windows Mobile 2003 for Pocket PC | 600MHz<br><br>Wi-Fi–enabled | Active Sync must be installed on your Pocket PC before you install Skype. |

Although you can run Skype on a computer that meets the minimum system requirements, the quality of the call depends on the performance of the computer, the speakers/microphone, and the speed of the Internet connection at both ends of the conversation.

Therefore, to get the best sound quality possible and to take advantage of the advanced Skype features, you will benefit from a powerful computer with a broadband connection, as well as a headset or handset with a built-in microphone.

## How Much Does Skype Cost?

Downloading, installing, and using Skype on a computer are free when you communicate with people who are also using Skype on their computers. Skype does charge for value-added services, however (such as SkypeIn and SkypeOut), and there are natural costs associated with the basic computer setup and network access needed to connect to the Internet and run Skype.

## Computer Connection and Headset Costs

To run Skype on a computer, you need a desktop, laptop, or Pocket PC device with sound capabilities, as well as a broadband connection. If you want to use Skype Video, you will also need a Webcam.

Skype works adequately on a 56K dial-up connection, but it is advisable to upgrade to a DSL, cable, or cellular broadband service to get the best possible sound. For minimum and recommended system requirements, refer back to Tables 3-1 and 3-2.

You also need a headset or speakers and a built-in or plug-in microphone. You can acquire a decent headset from the Skype Store or a retailer in the United States (such as Radio Shack) for as little as $12 U.S., and some people claim that the inexpensive headsets work as well as the more expensive ones on PCs.

Companies such as Plantronics and Logitech sell premium headsets with features like noise cancellation, higher-quality speakers, folding ability, and ergonomics in different styles at prices ranging from $12 to $75 U.S. Companies including Motorola sell wireless Bluetooth headsets for approximately $100 U.S.

Alternatively, you can use a handset like the Linksys cordless phone or the CyberPhone, which plugs into your computer's USB port. The USB handsets cost approximately $75 U.S., and the residential dual-mode cordless phones ring in at around $175 U.S. Again, you *do not* have to have a fancy or expensive headset to enjoy using Skype.

Webcams are available from companies such as Logitech, Creative Labs, and Hewlett-Packard. They range in price from $20 to $150 U.S., depending on image resolution and features.

## Skype-to-Skype Is Free

If you have access to the Internet, there is no charge for using Skype for voice calls, instant messaging, and transferring files between two Skype accounts (and for conference calls to up to five Skype accounts). Calls from one Skype account to another are always free.

## Voicemail

Skype offers free voicemail with a SkypeIn subscription, or a separate voicemail subscription for 3 months or 12 months. Currently, subscriptions are approximately $5 U.S. for three months and $15 U.S. for an annual subscription.

## Test Your Connection Speed (Optional)

If you plan to use Skype with a dial-up connection, it is highly recommended that you test your connection speed before you download and install Skype. If you find that your Internet connection speed is less than 56 kilobits per second (Kbps), consider upgrading to a broadband connection of at least 128 Kbps.

*Internet connection speed* refers to the rate of speed at which data transfers between the Internet and your computer. Put simply, it is the amount of time it takes your computer to download (or upload) a certain amount of data.

You can find any number of Web sites that offer tools for testing the speed of your Internet connection. The best way to find one is to use your favorite search engine and look for "testing Internet connection speed."

Internet-connection-speed tools allow you to see how fast your connection actually is, regardless of the type of connection you have, how fast the connection is rated, and the kind of computer you use to browse the Web.

Here are some popular Web sites that offer tools for testing your connection to the Internet:

- CNET—http://reviews.cnet.com/Bandwidth_meter/ 7004-7254_7-0.html
- Broadband Reports—www.dslreports.com/stest
- PC PitStop—www.pcpitstop.com/internet/default.asp

# Installing Skype on Microsoft Windows 2000/XP

To install Skype on your computer, you need to download the Skype application from the Skype Web site; save the installation file on your computer; and then begin the actual installation process, using an installation wizard that takes you through each step of the process.

This section discusses the steps for downloading and installing Skype on a Windows PC running Windows 2000, Windows XP Home Edition, or Windows XP Professional.

NOTE    You may notice minor differences between what is covered in this book and what you see during the installation process, because the Skype Web site, application software, and installation tasks are evolving continually to improve the Skype experience.

## Downloading Skype to Your Windows PC

To download Skype to your Windows PC, follow these steps:

1. Open Internet Explorer or your favorite Web browser, and enter **www.skype.com** in the address bar.

2. Click the **Download** link on the Skype Web site; click the **Windows** link; and click **Download Skype**.

   You will see the Skype for Windows Web page. Wait a moment, and under normal circumstances you will see the File Download window, which should display after 10 or 15 seconds.

   If the File Download window fails to display automatically, go ahead and click the Download **Skype for Windows** link.

3. When you see the File Download window, click **Save**, as shown in Figure 3-1.

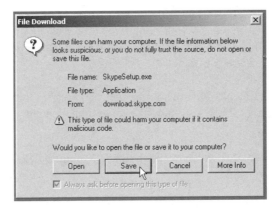

**Figure 3–1**   Downloading the Skype installer

4. Decide whether you want to use the default folder to save the Skype installation file that is about to be downloaded, and click **Save**, as shown in Figure 3-2.

   It does not matter where you save this file as long as you remember where it is. Common alternatives to the default location are the Windows Desktop or My Documents folder.

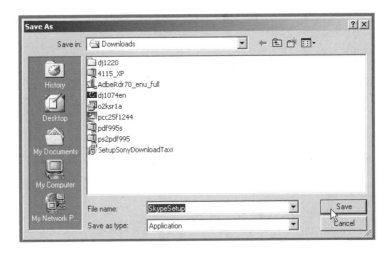

**Figure 3–2**   Saving the Skype installer on your computer

NOTE    Saving this installation file on your hard disk does not auto-matically install Skype on your computer. This file is simply a package that contains the Skype Setup Wizard, as well as all the necessary files that Skype needs to install.

NOTE    Downloading this installation file takes a few minutes. The 7MB file SkypeSetup.exe can take some time, depending on the speed of your Internet connection.

5. When you are ready to begin downloading the file to your com-puter, click **OK**.

When the download is complete, the installation may begin automat-ically. If it doesn't, close the File Download window. If the Skype Setup Wizard begins automatically, skip to step 2 in the next section to continue.

## Using the Skype Setup Wizard

To install Skype on your PC, follow these steps:

1. When you have closed the File Download window and are ready to install Skype, locate and double-click the Skype installation file, SkypeSetup.exe, that you just downloaded to your computer.

   You will see the Skype Setup Wizard.

2. Decide which language you prefer, and click **Next**.

3. Read the Skype license agreement; select **I Accept the Agree-ment** (see Figure 3-3); and click **Next**.

NOTE    Skype does not install any spyware, malware, or adware on your system.

WARNING    If you live in the United States, you need to be aware that Skype currently does not support 911 emergency calls. If you try to call 911 from Skype, you will not be connected.

4. Decide whether you want to use the default folder to install Skype on your computer or choose an alternative location; then click **Next**.

   By default, Skype chooses C:\Program Files\Skype\Phone. This is fine unless you have a reason to install it somewhere else.

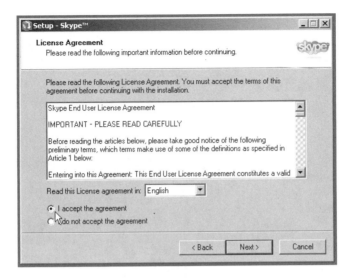

**Figure 3–3**   Accept the Skype license agreement

5. Choose which additional installation tasks should be performed (see Figure 3-4).

   • By default, Skype will start automatically and then run in the background when you turn on your computer. If your computer usually is connected to the Internet, this option is fine.

   If your computer generally is not connected to the Internet, do not have Skype start automatically, because when your computer boots up and is not connected to the Internet, Skype will continue trying to connect to the Internet until it succeeds or you quit the application.

   • Other options include creating a desktop icon and/or quick-launch icon. Choosing one or both of these options is fine. A desktop icon allows you to start Skype by clicking an icon on your desktop. A quick-launch icon displays in your Windows taskbar.

6. Click **Next**.

   The process of installing files on your hard disk should take less than a minute.

7. Complete the Skype Setup Wizard (see Figure 3-5).

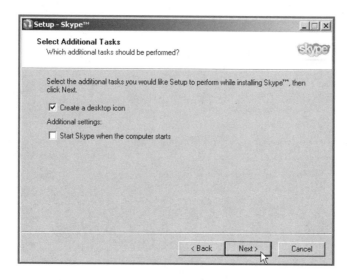

**Figure 3–4**    Choose additional installation tasks

**Figure 3–5**    Finish installation

8. If you are interested in late-breaking news about the version of Skype you are installing, or if you have previously installed Skype and are upgrading to a newer version, you may want to review the online release notes.

9. Complete the Skype installation by clicking **Finish**.

Now you're ready to create a new Skype account. You may want to install the optional Skype toolbar or jump directly to Chapter 4.

## Installing the Skype Web Toolbar (Optional)

You can install the optional Skype toolbar for Internet Explorer, Mozilla Firefox, or Outlook to streamline your Skype use and take advantage of enhanced Web-based Skype features. The Skype Web Toolbar lets you access Skype directly from Internet Explorer 5.0 or later, Firefox, or Outlook on a PC running Windows XP or Windows 2000.

The Skype toolbar allows you to:

- Launch various Skype functions from your browser window without having to open a Skype window. This means that from your browser, you can check to see which of your contacts is online, make calls, or start chats. You can also check your balances or go directly to the Skype Web site.

- Open a regular Web page and have Skype automatically identify any telephone numbers and convert them to SkypeOut links. You no longer have to leave your computer, pick up the phone, and dial a number.

To install the Skype Web Toolbar, you need to download the toolbar installation file from the Skype Web site, save the installation file on your computer, and then execute the installation process and toolbar configuration.

To install the Skype toolbar, follow these steps:

1. Open Internet Explorer or the Mozilla Firefox Web browser, and go to the Skype Web site.

2. Click the **Download** link; then click the **Skype for Windows** link.

   You see the Skype for Windows Web page.

3. Click the **Skype Web Toolbar** link; then click **Get It Now**.

4. Decide whether you want to use the default folder to save the Skype Web Toolbar installation file, which is about to be downloaded.

   It does not matter where you save this file, as long as you remember where it is. Common alternatives to the default location are the Windows Desktop or My Documents folder.

NOTE     Saving this installation file on your hard disk does not automatically install the Skype toolbar on your computer. This file is simply a package that contains all the necessary files that need to installed for the toolbar to work in concert with Skype.

5. When you are ready to begin downloading the file to your computer, click **OK**.

   Downloading this installation file is quick. The file can take from a few seconds to a few minutes to load over a broadband connection.

6. When the download is complete, close the File Download window, if it is still open; find the Skype toolbar installation file you just downloaded, and double-click it.

7. Read the Skype license agreement; select **I Accept the Agreement**; click **Next**; and continue until the installation is finished.

8. Close Internet Explorer Mozilla Firefox; then restart your browser.

   When you restart the browser, you will be notified that another program wants to use Skype, and you will be prompted to authorize the application.

9. Choose the option **Allow This Program to Use Skype All the Time**.

NOTE     Authorizing the application to use Skype only allows the browser toolbar to access Skype. It does not allow access from any other Web pages or scripts.

10. Configure the Skype Web Toolbar to select the locale (language), Internet Explorer, Mozilla Firefox behavior preferences, toolbar buttons, and default search engine.

You are done. Now you're ready to create a new Skype account. Skip to Chapter 4.

## Uninstalling Skype from Windows

You can uninstall Skype the same way that you uninstall any Windows software program. Follow these steps:

1. Choose Start > Control Panel or Settings > Control Panel.

2. Select Add/Remove Programs.

3. Select Skype.

4. Click Remove.

   The Skype application will be uninstalled.

# Installing Skype on Mac OS X

Downloading and installing Skype onto a Mac is simple and straightforward, assuming that you are running Mac OS X 10.3 or newer, have approximately 20MB of free space on your hard drive or *main volume,* and have a stable connection to the Internet.

To install Skype on your Mac, simply download the Skype application from the Skype Web site, open the mounted downloaded disk image on your Desktop, and then drag the Skype application from the mounted disk image volume to your Applications folder.

NOTE    There may be multiple places on the Skype home page where you can download the Skype application. The actual name of the button or link might be somewhat different, because Skype Technologies (the company) continually makes enhancements to the Skype Web site.

Here are the steps for downloading and installing Skype on a Mac using OS X:

1. Open Safari or your favorite Web browser, and enter **www.skype.com** in the address bar.

2. Click the **Download** link on the Skype Web site; then click any link that is appropriate for Mac OS X to begin downloading Skype

   Downloading this installation file takes a few minutes. The 7MB file Skype_number.dmg (where number is the version number) can take a little while, depending on the speed of your Internet connection.

   When downloading is complete, the Skype disk Image mounts on the Desktop, and a Finder window opens automatically, revealing the Skype application (see Figure 3-6).

3. Drag the Skype application to your Applications folder.

4. Drag the Skype application icon in your Applications folder to your Dock for convenient access to the Skype application.

5. In the Finder window, click the **Eject** button next to the mounted volume for Skype to eject the mounted volume from your Desktop.

   Next, you will need to create a new Skype account to register as a Skype user.

**Figure 3–6** Mac Finder window

6. Assuming that your Mac is still connected to the Internet, click the Skype application icon on your Dock or in the Applications folder to launch Skype and begin setting up your Skype account.

Now you're ready to create a new Skype account. Skip to Chapter 4.

## Uninstalling Skype from Mac OS X

You can uninstall Skype the same way that you uninstall any Mac OS X software program. To uninstall Skype from your Mac, follow these steps:

1. Go to the Applications folder.

2. Select the Skype application icon.

3. Drag the icon to the Trash.

4. Empty the Trash.

   Skype will be uninstalled.

# Installing Skype on Windows Mobile–Based Pocket PC

Downloading and installing Skype on a Pocket PC device is not difficult, assuming that you have a broadband Internet connection.

There are two methods for installing Skype on your Pocket PC:

- Download it directly to the Pocket PC device (preferred method).
- Download Skype to the PC and then install it on the Pocket PC device.

## Downloading Skype to the Pocket PC Device (Preferred Method)

The easiest way to install Skype on a device running Windows Mobile–based Pocket PC is to download the Cab installer for the handheld device directly from the Skype Web site, using the Web browser on the device. Installing Skype this way assumes that your Pocket PC device is able to connect wirelessly to the Internet.

To install Skype on your Pocket PC device using the preferred method, follow these steps:

1. If you have downloaded and successfully installed applications on your Pocket PC directly from the Internet before, here is the URL for downloading the Cab file:

   **www.skype.com/go/getskype-pocketpc-cab**

2. In the download window, check the **Open File after Download** checkbox, and click **Yes**.

3. Choose Start > File Explorer.

4. Click the Skype application icon.

Now you're ready to create a new Skype account or log into your existing account, if you have one. Skip to Chapter 4.

Otherwise, here are individual steps for downloading and installing Skype on a device running Pocket PC:

1. Open Internet Explorer on your Pocket PC device, and enter the following URL in the browser address bar:

   **www.skype.com/products/skype/pocketpc/**

2. Click the Cab Installer for Handheld Devices link, and click File Download.

   The download will start.

3. In the download window, check the **Open File after Download** checkbox, and click **Yes**.

   Installation will start automatically immediately after the download is complete.

4. When the installation is complete, go to Programs on your Pocket PC and click the Skype icon to start using Skype.

5. Complete the Skype installation by clicking **Finish**.

Now you're ready to create a new Skype account or log into your existing account, if you have one. Skip to Chapter 4.

## Downloading Skype to the PC First (Alternative Method)

Installing Skype on a Pocket PC device by downloading it to a PC requires that you have a broadband connection and have already installed Microsoft ActiveSync on the PC. Refer to your Pocket PC documentation for instructions on how to install and configure ActiveSync.

To install Skype on your PC and then your Pocket PC device, follow these steps:

1. Download the Skype application from this page on the Skype Web site:

   **www.skype.com/products/skype/pocketpc/**

2. Save the installation file to your PC.

3. When the file has downloaded completely, open the folder containing the file you downloaded; make sure that your Pocket PC device is connected to your computer with ActiveSync; and then double-click the installation file to start the installation.

4. Accept the Skype End User License Agreement.

   The ActiveSync Application Manager will pop up to copy the necessary files to your Pocket PC device.

## Uninstalling Skype from Pocket PC

You can uninstall Skype the same way that you uninstall any Pocket PC application:

1. Choose Start > Settings.

2. Select the System tab.

3. Select Remove Programs.

4. Select Skype.

5. Click Remove.

The Skype application will be uninstalled.

# Installing Skype on Linux

To install Skype on your Linux computer, you need to download the Skype application from the Skype Web site; save the `rpm` package or `tar` installation file on your hard disk; and then begin the actual installation process.

The process for installing Skype is being updated with each new version of Skype for Linux. Please check the Skype Web site for the most current installation instructions before you begin installing Skype for Linux.

Installing Skype on Linux assumes that:

• You are familiar with the Linux operating system.

• You have superuser `root` privileges on your computer.

If you are unfamiliar with Linux or do not have superuser privileges, consult your system administrator for assistance with downloading, installing, and configuring Skype.

Assuming that you are familiar with Linux, this section will take you through the steps for downloading and installing Skype on a PC running SuSE 9 or newer, Mandrake 10.1 or newer, Fedora Core 3 (Red Hat), or Debian-based Linux distributions.

**TIP**    If you have a Linux distribution other than the ones covered in this section, you may find it helpful to read this section and then go to the online Skype Forums (http://forum.skype.com).

**NOTE**    Although Skype for Linux works fine on many other distributions—including Gentoo, Sun Java Desktop System Release 2, and Red Hat 9—it is simply not feasible to cover the vast array of installation and configuration instructions in this book. There are too many variations related to hardware (32- versus 64-bit CPUs, sound cards and sound chips, and I/O devices) and software (OS distributions, kernel versions, sound drivers, desktop managers, and Linux sound-handling standards).

Here are some other key points that you may want to consider as you prepare to install and configure Skype for Linux:

**32-bit/64-bit hardware and OS**—Skype is a 32-bit application and is designed to run on i386-32 systems. Skype will run on a 64-bit CPU with a 64-bit version of Linux if you install the appropriate Qt 32-bit compatibility libraries and then run Skype within the

32-bit emulation layer. Refer to the Skype Forums at http://forum.skype.com for more information.

**KDE/GNOME desktop manager**—Skype supports both KDE and Gnome desktop managers.

**rpm/tar installation process**—You can install Skype using either rpm or tar, depending on your Linux distribution.

rpm provides the most convenient way to install software properly in the specific Linux systems for which the rpm software package was created. rpm stands for *Red Hat Package Manager*. It is the new standard Linux software package installer that originated with Red Hat Linux.

For the most current information on using Skype's apt and yum repositories, visit the Web page Skype for Linux Repositories (www.skype.com/products/skype/linux/repositories.html).

tar, which stands for *tape archive*, provides a universally accepted method for installing files manually wherever you like on your Linux system. tar is an operating system utility that people use for creating and unpacking compressed data archives.

- **Dynamic binaries** work on most Linux distributions as long as Qt version 3.2 or later and glibc 2.2.5 or later are installed. Qt is a graphical widget toolkit for developing programs with a graphical user interface.

- **Static binaries** have Qt compiled in and work on almost all distributions, including Red Hat 9. When you use the static binaries, Skype does not integrate automatically with your desktop-manager themes. And in some cases, you may need to install the appropriate dbus libraries, which you can get from your distribution media, the Web site for your Linux distribution, or from http://rpmfind.net. Be aware that you might also need Qt font and other configuration files installed for Skype to work properly.

**OSS/ALSA sound subsystem**—The sound system that Skype supports is the Open Sound System (OSS) standard using /dev/dsp as its audio input and output device. Skype works fine with the new Advanced Linux Sound Architecture (ALSA) standard when used in conjunction with the OSS emulation layer.

Since the 2.6 release of the Linux kernel, you may need to enable the ALSA driver for your sound card or chip for Skype to work properly. Refer to the ALSA sound card matrix in the online Skype Forums or the Web site for your Linux distribution for the most current information.

## Downloading Skype Using Linux

To download Skype to your Linux computer, follow these steps:

1. Point your favorite Web browser to the Skype Web site.

2. Click any button or links to download Skype for Linux, including **Download**.

   The Skype Downloads page is displayed.

3. Click the **Linux** link.

   The Download Skype for Linux page is displayed.

   Skype for Linux is available for a variety of Linux distributions, and it is available in both `rpm` and `tar` formats.

4. If you are new to the Linux operating system, find the appropriate `rpm` installation package for your version of Linux, regardless of whether it is Red Hat.

   If you are familiar with Linux and have previous experience using command-line tools, you may choose to download either the appropriate `rpm` installation or the `tar` file.

5. To begin downloading, click the appropriate link.

6. When you are given an opportunity to save the file to disk, do so.

7. Decide whether you want to use the default folder to save the Skype installation file that is about to be downloaded.

   By default, in most cases Linux will attempt to save the file in the home directory associated with the account on which you logged in.

   Downloading this installation file takes a few minutes. The approximately 7MB file can take a little while, depending on the speed of your Internet connection. The specific name of the installation file depends on the operating system distribution and type of installation you selected.

   NOTE   Saving this installation file on your hard disk does not automatically install Skype on your Linux computer. This file is simply a package that contains the Skype Setup Wizard as well as all of the necessary files that Skype needs to install.

8. When you are ready to begin downloading the file to your computer, click **OK**.

When downloading is complete, skip to "Installing Skype with rpm" or "Installing Skype with tar" later in this chapter.

## Installing Skype with rpm

The rpm installation process is simple and straightforward, as long as you have superuser root privileges and you are attempting to install Skype in one of the appropriate distributions and versions of Linux.

To install Skype on Linux using rpm, follow these steps:

1. Log in as the superuser root.

2. Navigate to the directory where you saved the rpm installation file.

   If you can't find the file you downloaded, open a terminal window, su to root, and update the list of files on your machine by typing

   **slocate -u**

   Then, at the root prompt #, search for the downloaded file by typing

   **slocate *skype-version.rpm***

3. Replace *skype-version.rpm* with the specific name of the file you downloaded.

   See the Skype for Linux Download Web page for the name of the file.

   Alternatively, you can use the find command at the root prompt # search for the downloaded file by typing

   **find / -name *skype-version.rpm* -print**

   Again, you need to replace *skype-version.rpm* with the specific name of the file you downloaded. See the Skype for Linux Download Web page for the name of the file.

4. Navigate to the directory where the slocate or find command found the Skype installation file, and begin the installation process by typing the following command:

   **rpm -Uvh *skype-version.rpm***

   Replace *skype-version.rpm* with the name of the file you downloaded—for example, skype-0_90_0_1.rpm. The -U flag tells the rpm command to install Skype and then delete any previously installed copies of the program. The -vh flag causes the system to display all installation messages to your monitor.

## Installing Skype with tar

The installation process using `tar` is straightforward, as long as you have superuser `root` privileges and you are attempting to install Skype in one of the appropriate distributions and versions of Linux.

To install Skype on Linux using `tar`, follow these steps:

1. Log in as the superuser `root`.

2. `cd` to the directory where you saved the `tar` file.

3. Enter the following command:

   **tar -xjvf *skype-version.tar.bz2***

   Replace *skype-version.tar.bz2* with the name of the file you downloaded, such as `skype-0_90_0_1.tar.bz2`.

   Skype is unpacked to the current directory.

NOTE     Unpacking a `tar` archive does not require `root` privileges. It requires only that you have appropriate permissions in the directory in which you unpack the `tar` archive.

## Configuring Linux for Skype

The following sections present several essential configuration changes you can make to optimize your chances of success using Skype with Linux.

## Run Skype with ALSA in OSS Emulation Mode

The recommended way to run Skype is with ALSA in OSS emulation mode.

This is because Skype relies on OSS and on being able to run in full-duplex mode. Most OSS drivers do not support full-duplex communication, however. As a result, they will crash the KDE `artsd` (Advanced Real-Time Synthesizer sound daemon) if you try to enable the driver to operate in full-duplex mode.

Be aware that you cannot enable both OSS and ALSA. You must disable OSS and then enable ALSA with OSS emulation. If, however, you choose to use an older OSS driver (and not the ALSA driver in OSS emulation mode), you may need to configure the driver to allow full-duplex communication.

Refer to Appendix C and the Unofficial Skype + Linux Sound FAQ on the Skype Forums for more information on configuring ALSA for OSS emulation.

## Set Nonblocking Mode in modules.conf

The default behavior for OSS is that the sound device is opened in blocking mode, which gives the application exclusive access to the device. Blocking mode can cause problems under certain circumstances. You can reconfigure ALSA to allow applications to open the sound device in nonblocking mode by appending the following command to your `modules.conf` file:

```
options snd-pcm-oss nonblock_open=1
```

## Start Skype Using KDE

If you plan to use the KDE desktop manager and have enabled system sound, you may need to edit your kmenu entry to make sure that when Skype launches, you can still play music and make calls at the same time.

To do this, edit your kmenu entry, and make sure that it contains this command:

```
artsdsp -m /usr/bin/skype
```

The `-m` option tells the system to use MMAP for memory-mapped sound.

For `artsdsp` to work properly with Skype, you may need to turn on full-duplex mode. To do this, choose Sound & Multimedia > Sound System. On the Hardware tab, make sure that the Full Duplex checkbox is checked and that the mixer is not muted.

## Verify Permissions for /dev/dsp

You can avoid the most common Skype installation problem by verifying that the permissions for `/dev/dsp` are set to read and write for the user who will be using Skype.

## Disable the Capture Channel on the Sound Card (or Chip)

Some sound cards and chips have a Capture channel set by default. To avoid hearing echoes on your calls, you may need to disable this Capture channel by starting your sound-mixer application and muting the capture channel.

## Run Skype on a Proxied Network

Skype for Linux might not connect if the Skype application is running on a proxied network. Skype supports regular HTTP or HTTPS proxies and authenticating HTTPS/SSL and SOCKS5 proxies. Skype for Linux automatically looks for proxy settings in Opera configuration files. You can set the appropriate environment variable `http_proxy` or `https_proxy` to point to the proxy (`host:port`).

## Uninstalling Skype from Linux

You can uninstall Skype the same way that you uninstall any Linux software program, depending on how the application was installed:

- If you used `tar` to install Skype, you can remove the Skype application and its associated directories with the `rm` command.
- If you installed Skype with `rpm`, you may want to refer to the documentation for your particular Linux distribution for specific instructions.

## Uninstalling Skype with tar

If you installed Skype with `tar`, uninstalling it requires great caution because you need to use the `rm` command, possibly as the superuser (`root`).

Because Skype has a daemon that runs as a background process, it is best to stop it before attempting to uninstall Skype.

To stop the process, first you must identify the process identification number. To do this, follow these steps:

1. Log in as the user who is running Skype, and type

   **ps -aux | grep skype**

2. When you have found the Linux process identification for the Skype application, kill the process by issuing the following command:

   **kill -9 *skype_process_ID***

   where *skype_process_ID* is the process identification number associated with Skype.

3. Change directories to the directory where `tar` was originally executed to install Skype.

   In other words, `cd` to the directory directly above the Skype directory.

4. When you are absolutely certain that you are in the correct directory, enter the following command to remove the Skype subdirectory and associated files forcefully:

   **rm -rf *skype-directory***

   where *skype-directory* is the specific name of the directory in which Skype is installed.

## Uninstalling Skype with rpm

If you installed Skype with rpm, uninstalling it is simple. You may want to check the man page for rpm on your Linux distribution to make sure that there is nothing special you need to know.

Because Skype has a daemon that runs as a background process, it is best to stop it before attempting to uninstall Skype. To stop the process, first you must identify the process identification number. To do this, follow these steps:

1. Log in as the user who is running Skype, and type

   **ps -aux | grep skype**

2. When you have found the Linux process identification number for the Skype application, kill the process by issuing the following command:

   **kill -9 *skype_process_ID***

   where *skype_process_ID* is the process identification number associated with Skype.

3. Enter the following command to uninstall the Skype application software:

   **rpm -e skype_package.rpm**

   where *skype_package* is the specific name of the rpm package that installed Skype—for example, skype-0_90_0_1.rpm.

In this chapter,
you learn how to:

Create a new Skype account

·

Set your preferences

·

Add contacts and Make a test call

·

Use Skype to make a call, send an
instant message (IM), and transfer a file

·

Configure your Skype preferences

# Details of Using Skype for the First Time

This chapter is designed for beginning computer users or for people who want detailed instructions for creating a Skype account and using Skype for the first time. This chapter covers the summarized material included in Chapter 2, but it offers more in-depth step-by-step instructions for other computer operating systems.

## Create a New Skype Account

When you have finished installing Skype, you will need to create a new Skype account and register as a Skype user. Setting up Skype account is simple, but the process varies slightly depending on whether you are a Microsoft Windows, Mac OS X, Pocket PC, or Linux user.

### Microsoft Windows

When you open Skype, you see the Sign in to Skype window. Because you don't yet have a Skype account, you will need to create one.

To create a Skype account, follow these steps:

1. In the Sign in to Skype window, click **Don't Have a Skype Name?** (see Figure 4-1).

   The Create a New Skype Account window is displayed (see Figure 4-2).

2. Enter a Skype Name in the required field.

   Your Skype Name must be unique. If you choose one that someone else has already registered, you will have the option of choosing an alternative name until you find one you like.

**Figure 4–1** Sign in to Skype window

**Figure 4–2** Create a New Skype Account window

3. To keep your account safe, enter a password in the required fields.

Your password must have six or more characters in it. You can change your password at any time when you have completed creating your new Skype account.

Here are some tips and tricks for choosing a password:

- Choose a password that is easy for you to remember but difficult for others to guess. Do not use obvious passwords such as the names of your children or family pet, for example.

- Create a memorable passphrase that includes uppercase and lowercase characters, symbols, and digits—for example, +IymCre8v2 (which says, "Plus I am creative too").

- Avoid using strings of numbers or text that might be available from an Internet search, such as your car's license plate number or other data that strangers might know about you.

- Do not write down your password (so choose one that is easy to remember).

- Do not tell anyone your password, including Skype staff members.

- Do not use a password that is in use somewhere else.

For more information on passwords and password strength, go to www.skype.com/security or www.getsafeonline.org.

4. Enter a valid e-mail address where Skype can send you a new password if you forget it.

If you forget your password and have not provided a valid e-mail address, there is no way to recover it. You will have to abandon your Skype Name and create a new Skype account. Skype will not send you any spam, and your e-mail address will not be displayed for others to see.

5. Verify that there is a check in the **Sign Me in When Skype Starts** checkbox.

When you do this, you will be logged on automatically when Skype starts. Logging in automatically saves you time every time. If you uncheck this checkbox, you will have to enter your Skype Name and password every time you start Skype. Leave this checkbox unchecked if you intend to use more than one Skype account and want to sign in with a different Skype Name when you start Skype.

6. Verify that there is a check in the **Start Skype When the Computer Starts** checkbox if you want Skype to launch automatically when you boot your computer.

7. Read the Skype end-user license agreement, and make sure that there is a check in the checkbox that indicates you accept it.

8. Click **Sign In**.

   You will see the Help Your Friends Find You window (see Figure 4-3). The information you enter here will help other Skype users search for you in the Skype public directory. You can always change this Personal Profile information later.

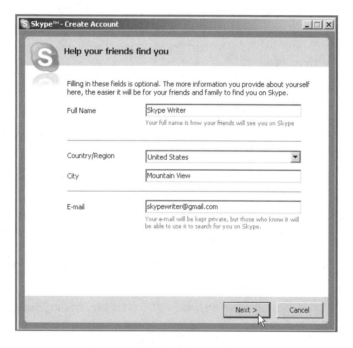

**Figure 4–3**   Help Your Friends Find You window

9. Fill in as many fields as you feel comfortable disclosing to others.

10. Verify your e-mail address.

Note    Your e-mail address is never displayed for others to see. E-mail addresses are used to allow you to reset your password if you forget it and to communicate with you about your account. If someone already knows your e-mail address and uses it to search for you in the Skype network, your information will be found, but your e-mail address will never be displayed.

11. Click **Next** to create your Skype account and register your Skype Name in the Skype network.

    This process may take a minute or so. If the Skype Name you chose was not unique, you can choose a variation of the name you wanted or try something different.

    You will see the Skype main window, shown in Figure 4-4 in the next section.

12. When you have familiarized yourself with the Skype main window, skip to "Make a Test Call" later in this chapter. Make sure that your headset or microphone is plugged into your computer, and get ready to begin using Skype.

If there is a problem connecting to the Internet, or if Skype experiences some type of error, see Chapter 7.

## Skype Main Window (Microsoft Windows)

The Skype user interface, or main window, shown in Figure 4-4, is organized around three main tabs:

- **Contacts** displays the Skype Names of the people in your Contacts List and each person's online status.
- **Dial** displays a keypad where you can dial a number directly when calling outside the Skype network.
- **History** shows a list of recent calls, chats, and file transfers you've made, as well as the dates and times of these communications. It also shows where you saved files that were transferred to your computer.

The top of the Skype main window also includes a series of action buttons; an events area, where you can see missed calls and received voicemails; and a services section, where you can get information about your Skype account. The bottom of the Skype main window contains a text box for entering Skype Names or phone numbers.

The Skype application works in a standard way across a variety of functions. Typically, you *select* one or more Skype Names and then *do* something (call, send an IM, start a conference call, or transfer a file).

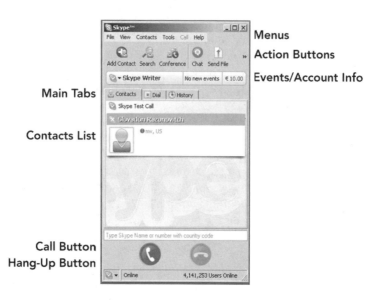

**Figure 4–4**   Skype main window for Microsoft Windows

## Mac OS X and Linux

When you open Skype, you will see the Sign in to Skype window. Because you don't yet have a Skype account, you will need to create one.

To create a Skype account, follow these steps:

1. Click **Create New Account**.

2. Enter a Skype Name in the required field.

   Your Skype Name must be unique. If you choose one that someone else has already registered, you will have the option of choosing an alternative name until you find one you like.

3. To keep your account safe, enter a password in the required fields.

   Your password must have six or more characters in it. You can change your password at any time when you have completed creating your new Skype account. For tips on choosing a password, refer to the Microsoft Windows section of "Create a New Skype Account" earlier in this chapter.

4. Enter a valid e-mail address.

   This e-mail address is used only for password recovery and to communicate with you about your account. It is essential that you enter a valid e-mail address. If you do not enter a valid e-mail address, and you forget your password, there will be no way to recover it, and you will have to abandon your Skype account and create a new one. Your e-mail address is never displayed for others to see.

5. Click the Skype license agreement; read it; and check the checkbox that indicates you have read the Skype license agreement and agree with its terms.

6. Decide whether you want to have Skype remember your name and password.

    If you uncheck this checkbox, you will have to enter your Skype Name and password every time you start Skype. You may want to leave this checkbox unchecked if you intend to use more than one active Skype account and want to sign in every time you launch Skype.

7. Decide whether you want to launch Skype when you log in.

    If your computer is not always connected to the Internet, you should uncheck this option. You can change this setting later.

8. Decide whether you want Skype to send you e-mail about new features, services, and other Skype-related information.

9. Click **Create** to create a new Skype account and register your Skype Name.

    This process may take a minute or so. If the Skype Name you chose was not unique, you can choose a variation of the name you wanted or try something different.

    You will see the Edit Profile window, shown in Figure 4-5. The information you enter here will help other Skype users search for you in the Skype network. You can always change this Personal Profile information later.

10. Fill in as many fields as you feel comfortable disclosing to others.

11. Add any e-mail address you think people may use to search for you on the Skype network.

NOTE    Your e-mail address is never displayed for others to see. If someone already knows your e-mail address and uses it to search for you in the Skype network, your information will be found, but your e-mail address will not be displayed.

12. Click **Apply**.

    You will see the Skype main window, shown in Figure 4-6 and Figure 4-7. If your main window does not look like this, choose **View > Show Toolbar** to display the action buttons.

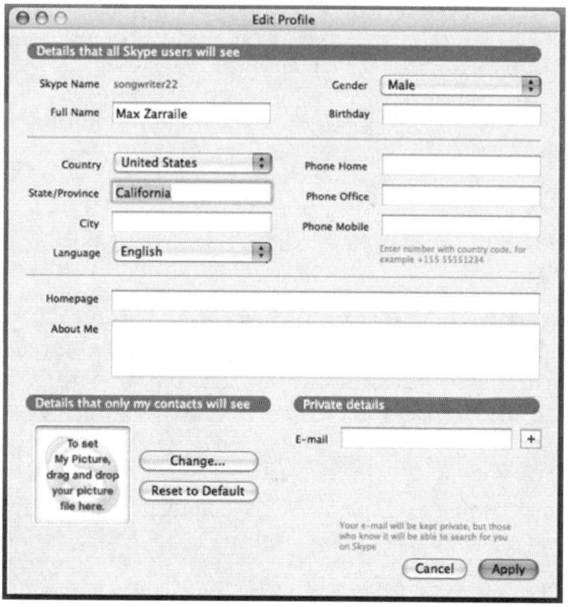

**Figure 4–5**   Edit Profile window for the Mac

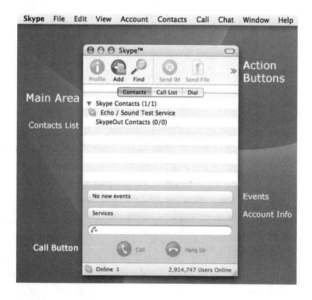

**Figure 4–6**   Skype main window for Mac OS X

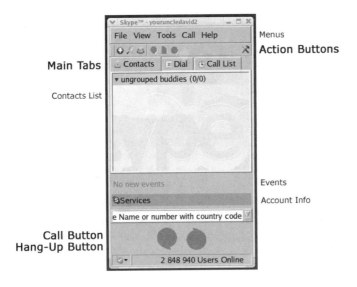

**Figure 4–7**   Skype main window for Linux

When you have familiarized yourself with the Skype main window, skip to "Make a Test Call" later in this chapter. Make sure that your headset or microphone is plugged into your computer, and get ready to begin using Skype.

If there is a problem connecting to the Internet, or if Skype experiences some type of error, see Chapter 7.

## Skype Main Window (Mac OS X and Linux)

The Skype user interface, or main window, is organized around three main sections:

- **Contacts** displays the Skype Names of the people in your Contacts List and each person's online status.
- **Call List** shows a list of recent calls, chats, and file transfers you've made, as well as the dates and times of these communications. It also shows where you saved files that were transferred to your computer.
- **Dial** displays a keypad where you can dial a number directly when calling outside the Skype network.

The top of the Skype main window also includes a series of action buttons. The bottom of the Skype main window contains an events area, where you can see missed calls and received voicemails; a services section, where you can get information about your Skype account; and a text box for entering Skype Names or phone numbers.

The Skype application works in a standard way across a variety of functions. Typically, you *select* one or more Skype Names and then *do* something (call, send an IM, start a conference call, or transfer a file).

## Pocket PC

When you open Skype, the first screen you see is the Skype End User License Agreement (EULA).

To create a new Skype account, follow these steps:

1. Read the EULA, if you like; scroll to the bottom of the document; and click **Accept**.

2. Click **Tap Here to Sign In**.

   Because you don't have a Skype account, you will need to create one.

3. Select the appropriate option, and click **OK**.

4. Enter a Skype Name in the required field.

   Your Skype Name must be unique. If you choose one that someone else has already registered, you will have the option of choosing an alternative name until you find one you like.

5. To keep your account safe, enter a password in the required fields.

   Your password must have six or more characters in it. You can change your password at any time when you have completed creating your new Skype account. For tips on choosing a password, refer to the Microsoft Windows section of "Create a New Skype Account" earlier in this chapter.

6. Enter a valid e-mail address.

   This e-mail address is used only for password recovery and to communicate with you about your account. It is essential that you enter a valid e-mail address. If you do not enter a valid e-mail address, and you forget your password, there will be no way to recover it, and you will have to abandon your Skype account and create a new one. Your e-mail address is never displayed for others to see.

NOTE    Your e-mail address is never displayed for others to see. If someone already knows your e-mail address and uses it to search for you in the Skype network, your information will be found, but your e-mail address will not be displayed.

7. Check the checkbox that indicates you have read the Skype license agreement and agree with its terms.

8. Click **OK** to create your Skype account and register your Skype Name in the Skype directory.

   This process may take a minute or so. If the Skype Name you chose was not unique, you can choose a variation of the name you wanted or try something different.

   You will see the Skype main window.

Skip to "Make a Test Call." Make sure that your headset or microphone is plugged into your computer, and get ready to begin using Skype. If there is a problem connecting to the Internet, or if Skype experiences some type of error, see Chapter 7.

# Make a Test Call

When you are done creating your new Skype account, it is a good idea to test your headset (or microphone and speakers) before you call someone. You can do this by making a test call to a special Skype answering service.

You will hear a recorded message, record your own voice, and listen back to it. Assuming that you have a connection to the Internet, here is how you make a test call:

1. Start Skype, if it is not already running.

2. Check that your headset, microphone (and speakers), or USB handset is plugged in properly.

   If you are using a microphone and speakers or a headset with 1/8-inch miniplugs, double-check that the microphone is plugged into the *input* jack and that the speakers (or headset) are plugged into the speaker *output* jack.

3. Enter **echo123** in the text box at the bottom of the Skype main window, and click the big green **Call** button (see Figure 4-8).

   Alternatively, in Microsoft Windows, you can choose **Tools > Options**, click **Sound Devices**, and then click **Make a Test Call to Skype Answering Machine**.

   If your speakers or headphones are working properly, you will hear ringing; then a prerecorded voice will ask you to leave a 10-second message.

4. Speak after the beep.

After 10 seconds, the message will be played back, assuming that everything is working properly. If you hear the prerecorded message and also your own recorded voice, you can safely assume that Skype is working properly.

**Figure 4–8**   Calling echo123

If Skype is not working properly, you can do some things to remedy the situation before you attempt to use Skype:

- **If you hear nothing:** Check to make absolutely sure that your headset or microphone is plugged into the correct jack and that your audio volume or volume control is set appropriately (not muted). Try making a test call again. If you still hear nothing, refer to Chapter 7 for more guidance and information.

- **If you hear something:** If you hear the prerecorded voice but cannot hear your own voice in the playback, you need to make sure that your microphone is working or adjust the recording settings. See the next section, "Testing Your Microphone."

NOTE     To adjust the volume on your speakers, headset, or handset, start by adjusting the output volume (sound volume) in the Sound Control Panel or System Preferences for your operating system.

# Testing Your Microphone

The most straightforward way to test your microphone is to use your microphone to record a sound (and listen to the recording).

NOTE    To adjust the volume of your microphone, speakers, or headset, go to the Sound Control Panel for your operating system. In Windows, choose Start > Settings > Control Panel > Sounds and Audio Devices. (Mac OS X users, choose Apple > System Preferences > Sound.)

## Microsoft Windows

To test your microphone, follow these steps:

1. Choose Start > Programs.

2. Find the Entertainment section of the Accessories menu, and click Sound Recorder.

3. When the Sound Recorder panel is displayed, try to record your speech through the microphone.

4. Try to play your recording back.

5. If you still can't hear your recording, go the Sounds and Audio section of Control Panel and try adjusting the microphone settings until the recording test works, or refer to Chapter 7 for additional help.

## Mac OS X

To test your microphone, follow these steps:

1. Choose Apple > System Preferences.

2. Select Audio.

3. Make sure that the appropriate microphone is selected; adjust the input level so that it registers your voice at approximately 75 percent; and see whether the input level changes when you speak into the microphone.

4. To adjust the volume of your speakers or headset, use your keyboard audio control, or choose System Preferences > Audio and increase the output volume.

   Make sure that the output volume is not muted.

5. If you do not see the appropriate microphone, headset, or handset displayed, try disconnecting and reconnecting it; if that doesn't work, refer to Chapter 7 for assistance.

## Pocket PC

To test your microphone, try recording a voice memo using Pocket PC's built-in voice recorder. Record a voice memo and then try playing it back.

## Linux

To test your microphone, follow these steps:

1. Depending on the version of Linux you are using, go to the Programs section of the desktop manager menu.

2. Find the Sound & Video section of the menu, and click Sound Recorder.

3. When the Sound Recorder panel is displayed, try to record your speech through the microphone you use.

4. Try to play your recording back.

5. If you still can't hear your recording, go the Sounds and Audio section of Control Panel and try adjusting the microphone settings until the recording test works, or refer to Chapter 7 for additional help.

# Add Contacts

*Contacts* are people in the Skype network with whom you want to communicate. Your Contacts List will be empty when you first start Skype, so you will need to add contacts before you can make a call (or send an IM or transfer a file). You can add contacts in two ways:

- **Search:** Use Skype to search the network for names of people you may know. When the search is complete, you can select a Skype Name and add it to your Contacts List.

- **Import:** Let Skype automatically scan for contacts in Microsoft Outlook, Outlook Express, Opera, and MSN Messenger. When the scan is complete, you can select a Skype Name and add it to your Contacts List.

## Microsoft Windows

To add a contact to your Contacts List, follow these steps:

1. Click the **Add Contact** icon in the Skype main window (see Figure 4-9).

**Figure 4–9**   Add a contact

2. Type the Skype Name, full name, or e-mail address, and click **Search**.

   Skype will search the database to validate that the user exists.

   NOTE    The person you are looking for may not be in the directory if he hasn't used Skype for a while. You may want to reach him by other means to get his Skype name.

3. Select a contact from the list, and click **Add Selected Contact** (see Figure 4-10).

   You will be asked to send your contact details. Skip to step 4.

Alternatively, you can click the **Search** icon and enter additional search criteria:

- Type the Skype Name, full name, or e-mail address of the person you are looking for, and click **Search**.

- Select a contact from the list, and click **Add Selected Contact**. You will be asked to send your contact details.

Alternatively, you can use Skype's ability to import contacts from address books in Outlook or other programs. To do this, choose **Contacts > Import Contacts**. Skype will search your address book and compare the information it finds with Skype Names. If Skype discovers any matches, you can follow the wizard to import contacts.

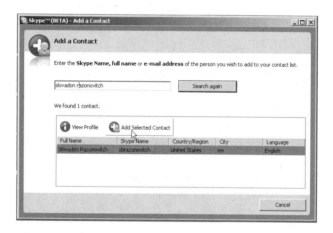

**Figure 4–10**   Add a selected contact

4. Send your details (request other's details).

When you add a new contact, you will see the Send Your Details window, allowing you to notify the contact that he or she has been added to your Contacts List (see Figure 4-11). You can also choose whether you want this person to see your contact details, such as your full name and online status. (*Online status* lets other Skype users know when you are online and available for communicating.)

When you allow someone to see your contact details, you *authorize* her to see your details. You can set your Skype security preferences to prevent people you have not authorized to see your contact details from contacting you.

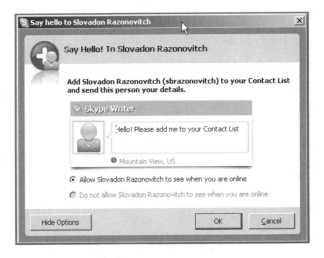

**Figure 4–11**   Send your contact details

5. Type a message (optional), specify whether you would like to share your contact details with this person or keep them private, and click **OK**.

   The person receiving your message will have a chance to share his details. Depending on how this user has configured his privacy settings, you might not be able to contact this person until he has authorized you to see his own contact details.

   TIP    If you need to send another request to this person in the future, you can right-click the Skype Name and select Request Contact Details from the context menu.

   NOTE    When you have authorized someone to see your contact details, you cannot revoke the authorization. You can block a user from contacting you, however. See Chapter 5 for more information.

## Mac OS X

There are two ways to add a contact to your Contacts List.

The simplest way is to use the **Add** icon if you know the exact spelling of the person's Skype Name.

If you are unsure of the spelling, or if you want to search the Skype network by using a person's name, e-mail address, or other information in her profile, use the **Find** icon.

To search the Skype network, follow these steps:

1. Click the **Find** icon or choose **Contacts > Search for People**.

2. Type the name of the person you want to add to your Contacts List, and click **Find**.

   Skype will search the network and display a list of matches (see Figure 4-12).

   If multiple matches are displayed, you can select a contact and click the **Profile** icon in the search-results box to determine whether this is the person you want to add.

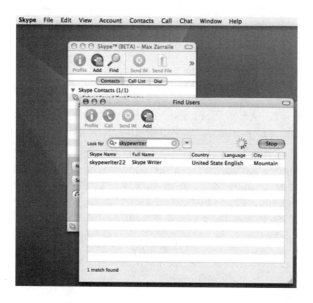

**Figure 4–12** Search results

3. To add a contact to your Contacts List, make sure that the correct contact is selected; and click the **Add** icon.

   Alternatively, you can use Skype's ability to import contacts from your address book in Entourage or other programs. To do this, choose **Contacts > Import from Address Book**. Skype will search your address book and compare the information it finds with Skype Names. If Skype discovers any matches, you can follow the wizard to import contacts.

4. Complete an authorization request.

   When you add a new contact, you will be asked to complete an authorization request. This allows you to make a request to see the online status of the person you are adding. This also allows you to specify whether you want your new contact to see your online status (see Figure 4-13).

   Authorizations are designed as part of Skype's privacy configurations. You can set your Skype preferences to allow calls from anyone, only from people in your Contacts List, or only from people you have authorized.

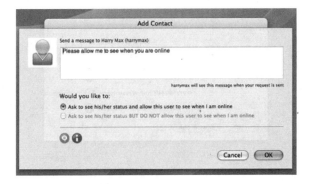

**Figure 4–13** Authorization (for Mac)

5. Type a message (optional).

6. Select an option to allow or disallow the contact to see when you are online, and click **OK**.

   The person receiving the authorization will need to accept it for you to be able to see his online status. Depending on how this user has configured his privacy settings, you might not be able contact this person until you have been authorized.

TIP    If you need to send another request to this person in the future, you can Control-click the Skype Name and select Request Authorization from the context menu.

NOTE    When you have authorized someone to see your online status, you cannot revoke the authorization. You can block a user from contacting you, however. See Chapter 5 for more information.

7. Click **OK**. When the contact has been added, you can call the contact, send an IM, or add more contacts.

# Set Your Skype Preferences

Skype offers a variety of settings and options so you can customize your Skype to suit your habits and needs. Preferences are a host of options, including general operations, privacy, notifications, sound alerts, sound devices, connection options, and voicemail.

By default, the preferences are already set to satisfy most people. You can change your preferences at any time, and you may want to change some preferences beyond the basic settings covered in this section. You will find a detailed summary of the Skype preference menus and settings at the end of this chapter.

## Microsoft Windows Preferences

To set your preferences, follow these steps:

1. In the Skype main window, choose **Tools** > **Options**.

   The Options window appears (see Figure 4-14).

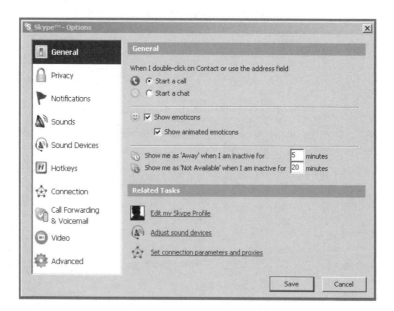

**Figure 4–14** Options window/General options

To exit a menu, click **Cancel**. To save any changes, click **Save**. The changes will be adopted immediately. If you make a mistake, simply go back to the menu, change the settings again, and click **Save**.

2. Select the **General** menu at the top of the list (if it is not already selected).

3. Decide whether you want Skype to start a call or start a chat (IM session) when you double-click a contact; specify whether you want to use emoticons; and set your preferences for 'Away' and 'Not Available.'

   'Away' and 'Not Available' represent a user's online status. Skype displays icons showing your online status so that other Skype users can know whether you are online and whether they can contact you.

   The double-click preference is a personal choice, and it depends on how you prefer to use Skype. Whereas many Skype users prefer to set this option to start a conversation by chatting (instant messaging), others prefer to start talking immediately.

4. Click **Save** to save your changes.

5. Select the **Privacy** menu.

6. Decide whom you want to be allowed to call and chat with you.

   When you are first using Skype, you may want to allow anyone to call or chat. You can change these preferences at any time. If you are sure that you do not want people you may not know contacting you, opt to allow only the people from your Contacts List or only those with whom you have shared your contact details.

7. Select the **Notifications** menu.

8. Select when you want to be notified of an event with a small pop-up menu, and click **Save** to save your changes.

9. Select the **Sounds** menu.

10. Specify when you want to be alerted of an event with a sound, and click **Save** to save your changes.

    To hear the default sound, click the green **Play** button.

    • If you do not want to be alerted of an event, uncheck the **Play Sound** checkbox for a particular event.

    • To upload a sound file of your own, click **Import Sounds**; select a .wav file from your collection; and click **Open**.

11. Select the **Sound Devices** menu.

12. Click **Let Skype Adjust My Sound Device Settings** or **Specify Each Device**.

13. Check the **Ring PC Speaker** checkbox to have Skype ring your speakers even if you have a headset plugged in, and click **Save** to save your changes.

14. Repeat these instructions for any of the other types of preferences you want to set.

NOTE    Because Skype users who have purchased voicemail can leave voicemail messages (even if *you* have not purchased a subscription to voicemail), you should record a welcome message (personal greeting). Your welcome message is located in the Call Forwarding & Voicemail menu.

## Mac OS X Preferences

To set your preferences, follow these steps:

1. In the Skype main window, choose **Skype** > **Preferences**.

   The Options window is displayed.

2. Select the **General** menu (if it is not already selected).

3. Decide whether you want Skype to start a call or start instant messaging when you double-click a contact, and set your preferences for 'Away' and 'Not Available.'

   'Away' and 'Not Available' represent a user's online status. Skype displays icons showing your online status so that other Skype users can know whether you are online and whether they can contact you.

   The double-click preference is a personal choice, and it depends on how you like to begin communicating with people. Whereas many Skype users prefer to set this option to start a conversation by instant messaging, others want to start talking immediately.

4. Select the **Privacy** menu.

5. Decide whom you want to be allowed to call and chat with you, and decide whom you want to be able to see your picture, should you choose to include one in your profile.

   When you are first using Skype, you may want to allow anyone to call or chat. You can change any preferences at any time. If you are sure that you do not want people you may not know contacting you, opt to allow only the people from your Contacts List or only those you have authorized.

6. Select the **Events** menu.

7. Make sure that there is a check in the **Bounce Icon in the Dock** checkbox.

    It's a good idea to check the **Repeat** box. The bouncing Dock is the only visual indicator you have, and having the bounce repeat can be helpful when the volume is turned down low or you are using a headset but not wearing it.

8. Repeat these instructions for any of the other types of preferences you want to set.

NOTE    Because Skype users who have purchased voicemail can leave voicemail messages (even if you have not purchased a subscription to voicemail), you should record a personal greeting using the Voicemail menu.

## Pocket PC Preferences

To set your preferences, follow these steps:

1. In the Skype main window, choose **Tools** > **Options**.

2. Decide whether you want Skype to start a call or start a chat (IM session) when you double-click a contact, and set your preferences for 'Away' and 'Not Available.'

    'Away' and 'Not Available' represent the user's online status. Skype displays icons showing your online status so that other Skype users can know whether you are online and whether they can contact you.

3. Select your preferred language.

4. Decide whom you want to allow to call and IM (chat with) you.

    When you are first using Skype, you may want to allow anyone to call or chat. You can always change these preferences at any time. If you are sure that you do not want people you may not know contacting you, opt to allow only the people from your Contacts List or only those you have authorized.

5. Decide whether you want to prevent your Pocket PC device from going into standby mode while you are online with Skype.

6. If you do not plan to use a headset with your Pocket PC device, check the **Echo Cancellation ON** checkbox.

7. Click **OK** to save your preferences.

## Linux Preferences

To set your preferences, follow these steps:

1. In the Skype main window, choose **Tools** > **Options**.

    Generally, Skype users find the default settings are adequate and do not need to be adjusted.

2. Select the **General** menu at the top of the list (if it is not already selected).

3. Decide whether you want Skype to start a call or start a chat (IM session) when you double-click a contact; set your preferences for 'Away' and 'Not Available'; and click **Save** to save your changes.

    'Away' and 'Not Available' represent a user's online status. Skype displays icons showing your online status so that other Skype users can know whether you are online and whether they can contact you.

4. Select the **Privacy** menu.

5. Decide whom you want to be allowed to call and IM (chat with) you.

    When you are first using Skype, you may want to allow anyone to call or chat. You can always change these preferences at any time. If you are sure that you do not want people you may not know contacting you, opt to allow only the people from your Contacts List or only those you have authorized.

6. Specify how long you want your chat histories kept, and click **Save** to save your changes.

    Chat histories are saved locally on your computer and you can view a log of your messages if you choose to save the chat history.

7. Select the **Call Alerts** menu.

8. Specify how and when you want to be alerted in the event of an incoming call.

    Select **Ring PC Speaker** to have Skype ring your speakers even if you have a headset plugged in, for example.

9. Select the **Chat Alerts** menu.

10. Specify how and when you want to be alerted in the event of an incoming chat; then click **Save** to save your changes.

11. Repeat these instructions for any of the other types of preferences you want to set.

# Make a Call

There are three simple ways to make a call using Skype:

- Select a Skype Name in your Contacts List and then click the big green **Call** button in the bottom-left portion of the Skype main window (see Figure 4-15).

**Figure 4–15**    Making a call with the Call button

- Right-click a Skype Name in your Contacts List, and choose **Start Call** from the context menu (see Figure 4-16). (Mac users: Control-click the Skype Name, and choose **Call** from the context menu.)

- Double-click the Skype Name in your Contacts List or search results (if you have set your Skype preferences to initiate a call versus an IM).

NOTE    You can also make a call to someone using a cell phone or a traditional phone. To do this, you need to buy SkypeOut credits. See Chapter 5 for more information.

**Figure 4–16**    Making a call with the Call menu

# End a Call

You can end a call at any time simply by clicking the big red **Hang Up** button in the bottom-right portion of the Skype main window (see Figure 4-17). You can also end a call from the **Call** menu.

**Figure 4–17**    Hang Up button

# Receive a Call

When someone is calling, Skype will alert you with the sound of a ringing telephone. Click the big green **Call** button to answer the call. Click the big red **Hang Up** button to reject it.

# Start a Chat (Send an Instant Message)

The procedure for starting a chat is very similar to making a call.
   To send an IM (start a chat), follow these steps:

1. Select a Skype Name in your Contacts List and then click the **Chat** icon in the Skype main window (see Figure 4-18).

   (Mac users: Select a Skype Name, and click the **Send IM** icon.)

**Figure 4–18**   Contact with Chat icon

2. Right-click a Skype Name in your Contacts List, and choose **Start Chat** from the context menu (see Figure 4-19).

(Mac users: Control-click the Skype Name, and choose **Send Instant Message** from the context menu.)

**Figure 4–19**  Contact with Chat menu

3. Double-click the Skype Name in your Contacts List (if you have set your Skype preferences to initiate an instant IM versus start a call).

# Transfer a File

The way you transfer a file is also similar to the way you make a call or send an IM.

To transfer a file, follow these steps:

1. Select a Skype Name in your Contacts List and then click the **Send File** icon.

2. Right-click a Skype Name in your Contacts List, and select **Send File** from the context menu (see Figure 4-20).

   (Mac users: Control-click the Skype Name, and choose **Send File** from the context menu.)

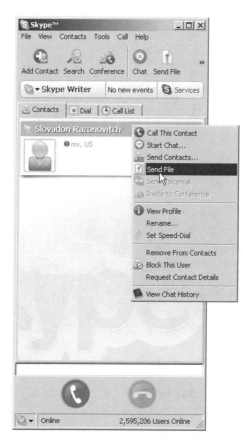

**Figure 4–20**   Transfer with Send File menu

You can send files only to people who have authorized you to see their contact details, and the recipient of the file transfer must be online to accept the transfer before it can go through.

3. If you need to request someone's details, right-click the contact, and select **Request Contact Details** from the context menu.

(Mac users: Control-click the contact, and select **Request Authorization** from the context menu.)

NOTE   Skype allows system administrators to disable the file-transfer capability. If the Skype application user interface for transferring files is grayed out, it means that someone has configured your Skype application to prevent you from sending or receiving files in this fashion. Refer to Appendix B or consult your system administrator for clarification or help.

# Your Personal Profile

When you created your Skype account and entered any optional information to help your friends find you, you created the beginnings of your Personal Profile. Your Personal Profile contains information that allows other users to find your Skype Name on the Skype network. When you add information to your profile, you are making it available to the Skype network—with the exception of your e-mail address. Your e-mail address is always kept private.

## View a Profile

There are two reasons why you may want to view somebody's profile. The first reason is to verify who someone is before you add her to your Contacts List. The second reason is to determine who someone is before you answer a call or start a chat session.

To view a Skype user's profile before adding him to your Contacts List, select the person's Skype Name from the search results, and click the **Profile** icon. A Profile window is displayed, as shown in Figure 4-21.

To view a profile while someone is calling, click the **Profile** icon. (Mac users: Choose **Advanced** > **View Profile**, as shown in Figure 4-22.)

## Update Your Own Profile

To update your profile, choose **File** > **Edit My Profile**. Add or change details to your profile as appropriate. (Mac users: Choose **Account** > **My Profile**.)

**Figure 4–21**   Profile information

**Figure 4–22**   View profile during a call (Mac)

You also have the option of selecting a picture or uploading a bitmap or .JPEG file from your files. This picture is what callers will see when they Skype you.

To select a picture from a list, follow these steps:

1. Click the **Change** button in the **My Profile** window.

2. Select a picture, and click **OK**.

   Alternatively, you can click Get New Pictures to buy a photo from the Skype Web site.

To upload an image from your files, follow these steps:

1. In the My Profile screen, click the **Change** button.

2. Click **Browse** to select a photo of your own.

3. Select the folder on your computer that holds your photo; click the name of the photo; and click **Open**.

   You should see the photo in the list.

4. Select the photo, and click **OK**.

To verify that the new icon or photo is now in your Personal Profile, choose **File** > **Edit My Profile**. (Mac users: Choose **Account** > **My Profile**.)

# Summary of Preference Menus

Skype allows you to set your preferences to customize how Skype works. To display the preference menus, choose **Tools** > **Options**. (Mac users: Choose **Skype** > **Preferences**.)

## Microsoft Windows Preferences Menu Summary

**General**—When you click a contact, do you want Skype to start a chat or a call? How long do you want Skype to wait before changing your status to unavailable? Here are the general preferences you can set:

- **When I Double-Click a Contact.** Determines whether double-clicking a contact initiates a chat session or a voice call. This is a personal preference.

- **Show Emoticons.** This preference lets you send and receive graphical emotions in text messages. And it translates text emoticons, such as a smile or wink ;-) into a small graphical face with a wink gesture. Animated emoticons are moving graphical emotions. The choice to show emoticons is a very personal one. There is no general rule for making a decision about whether to show them.

- **Show Me 'Away' and Show Me As 'Not Available.'** This option informs the Skype application to change your online status indicator automatically, depending on how long it has been since you have touched your computer.

Related tasks provide shortcuts to other things you might want to do, such as edit your Skype profile or adjust sound devices. Network administrators can also adjust connection parameters and proxy settings.

**Privacy**—Who do you want to be able to call you? Who do you want to be able to send you IMs? Although these options may seem self-evident, typically, Skype users set them as follows:

- **Allow Calls From:** Only people from my Contacts List
- **Allow Chats From:** Anyone
- **Keep Chat History:** Forever

How you set the chat-history preference depends on your particular need for security and privacy. If you have particular concerns about where Skype stores chat-history information, refer to the section in Appendix B on where sensitive data is stored for more information.

**Manage Blocked Users**—This feature allows you to specify Skype Names that you want to block (or unblock) from contacting you under any circumstances.

**Notifications**—This feature lets you specify when you want your computer to display an alert that something of interest has happened. Do you want to know when one of your contacts comes online, for example? These preferences should seem self-evident, and by default, they are all turned on. If, over time, you find that certain notifications become distracting, you can always turn them off.

**Sounds**—This feature lets you specify when your computer should play a sound to notify you that something interesting has happened. You can upload your own sounds in the form of .WAV files or mute all sounds, if necessary. Do you want to hear a ring when somebody is calling? When the other party is busy? When the other party hangs up? Like Notifications, these preferences should seem self-evident, and by default, they are turned on. If any of them becomes distracting, you can always turn one or more of them off.

**Sound Devices**—This feature lets you fine-tune or override your computer's audio settings as they relate to Skype. When you are using one sound device (such as a headset or one microphone and one set of speakers), the default settings work best. They are

- **Audio In:** Windows Default Device
- **Audio Out:** Windows Default Device
- **Ringing:** Windows Default Device

- **Ring PC Speaker:** On (check)
- **Let Skype Adjust My Sound Device Settings:** On (check)

**Hotkeys**—This feature allows you to configure keyboard short-cuts for answering calls, rejecting calls, muting, searching, and other actions you perform frequently. In addition, you will find an option to change the way that Skype treats the Enter key in a chat session. By default, Skype sends a chat message when you press Enter. You can change the option, however, so that pressing Enter puts a line break between paragraphs, which is important for people who type very long messages. If you change this chat setting, you will need to click the carriage-return icon in the chat window (or press Alt+S) to send the message.

**Connection**—This feature gives network administrators control to configure network communication settings such as ports, proxy detection, and proxy authentication. Do not change these settings without consulting a system administrator.

These preferences allow system and network administrators to change the incoming connection port:

- **Port for Incoming Connections:** Set to 0 by default
- **Use Port 80 and 443 As Alternatives for Incoming Connections:** Selected by default

These port settings configure Skype to "listen" for incoming communications from other Skype users—that is, assuming that the data is not blocked by a firewall. Skype does not send outgoing UDP packets from this port. As a result, this port setting does not affect outgoing communications or your ability to connect with the Skype network and other Skype users.

**Call Forwarding and Voicemail**—Do you want your calls to be forwarded to a traditional phone when you're not on Skype? If so, you can configure Skype to forward such calls, provided that you have sufficient SkypeOut credit. In addition, you can record a standard voicemail greeting. You have additional options if you subscribe to voicemail or have purchased a SkypeIn number that came with voicemail.

**Video**—This feature lets you enable or disable Skype video. Do you want Skype video to start automatically when you are on a call? From whom do you want to receive video calls? Do you want others to know that you have Skype video?

**Advanced**—This feature provides options for startup, call, chat, and other preferences that are rarely changed after they are set. Do you want Skype to launch when you start your computer and log in? When you click a contact, do you want Skype to start a chat or a call? How long do you want Skype to wait before changing your status to 'Away' or 'Not Available'?

- **Start Skype When I Start Windows.** This is a good option to turn on if your computer is always connected to the Internet. Otherwise, you will find it more convenient to launch Skype manually when the connection to the Internet has been established.

- **Check for Updates Automatically.** This option is a great way to stay up to date with the latest version of Skype. If there are updates, you will get an alert.

- **Automatically Answer Incoming Call.** This option allows you to make sure that you don't miss a call if you are busy working on your computer and need extra time to answer calls.

- **Set Chat Style.** This option really depends on how you prefer to use Skype. Although many Skype users prefer to leave the default setting alone, people who have used the IRC chat system for a long time may prefer to alter how Skype presents chat sessions.

- **Show Timestamp with Chat Messages.** Most Skype users have no preference as to whether this setting should be on or off. By default, chat messages are timestamped for convenience.

- **Pop up a Chat Window When Someone Starts to Chat with Me.** This is another setting that depends on how you prefer to use Skype. Most Skype users prefer to leave the default setting alone, which causes a new window to pop up when someone begins to chat.

- **Automatically Pop up Requests for Contact Details.** This option generates a pop-up window every time a Skype user requests your contact details.

- **Associate Skype with Callto: Links.** This preference allows Skype to recognize special links on Web pages that are designed to support Internet phone calls. By default, Skype allows you to initiate a call simply by clicking these types of links. If you change this setting, Skype will no longer automatically associate these special callto: links with the Skype application.

- **Automatically Pause Winamp During Calls.** This option lets you configure your PC to prioritize Skype calls over all other audio activity and events that could interrupt you during a call. If you check this checkbox, Skype sound will take precedence over all non-Skype audio alerts and sound events (such as music playing). Most people simply want to be able to turn the volume of the music down manually, so by default, this check-box is unchecked.

- **Display Technical Call Information.** Network administrators, and software and hardware developers may use this option to analyze information about Skype calls.

## Mac OS X Preferences Menu Summary

**General**—Do you want Skype to launch when you start your computer and log in? When you click a contact, do you want Skype to start a chat or a call? How long do you want Skype to wait before changing your status to unavailable?

- **Launch Skype When I Log In** starts Skype at login time. This is a good option if your computer is always connected to the Internet. Otherwise, it's more convenient to launch Skype manually when the connection to the Internet has been established.

- Choose **Remember My Name and Password on This Computer** only if you are the only person who uses the computer or if you have a separate login. Otherwise, other people who use the computer may inadvertently use your Skype account.

- **Check for Updates Automatically** is a great way to stay up to date with the latest version of Skype.

- **When I Double-Click a Contact** determines whether double-clicking a contact initiates a chat session or a voice call. It's your choice, and it's a personal preference.

- **Save Received Files** tells Skype where to put files that you receive. Use the default location unless you prefer to save them in a different location.

- **Show Me 'Away'** and **Show Me As 'Not Available'** inform the Skype application to change your online status indicator automatically, depending on how much time has passed since you have interacted with your computer.

**Privacy**—Who do you want to be able to call you? To whom do you want to be able to send IMs? Who do you want to be able to use your SkypeIn number? How long do you want your chat history kept? Although these options may seem self-evident, typically, Skype users set them as follows:

- **Allow Calls From:** Only people from my Contacts List
- **Allow Instant Messages (Chat) From:** Anyone
- **Allow SkypeIn Calls From:** Anyone
- **Show My Picture To:** Anyone

- **Enable Bonjour:** Off (no check). The Apple network service, formally known as Rendezvous, provides a novel way to discover services on a local-area network.

**Manage Blocked Users**—This feature allows you to specify Skype Names that you want to block (or unblock) from contacting you.

**Events**—How do you want Skype to treat pop-up windows, sounds, and other system behaviors to alert you to the fact that something of interest has happened? The default settings generally are fine, but you can fine-tune them, if you like. You can even add your own sounds. When a call comes in, do you want a sound to play? Do you want to bounce the Skype icon in the Dock? Do you want to be notified when one of your contacts comes online or starts a chat with you? Sends you a file? Requests authorization? Sends you contacts? Leaves you voicemail? Do you want your Mac to tell you with spoken text?

**Audio**—This feature allows you to fine-tune or override your computer's audio settings as they relate to Skype.

**Calls**—This feature allows you to record your voicemail greeting, send calls to voicemail (when rejected) or play the busy signal, record a welcome message (must have voicemail subscription or SkypeIn number), specify the amount of time that should pass before Skype sends a call to voicemail, and forward unanswered calls to one or more numbers. Forwarded calls are sent to all numbers simultaneously, and each forwarded call will be charged separately as a SkypeOut call.

**Chat**—These options are the basic options for setting chat preferences. Most Skype users prefer to leave the default settings alone:

- **Open Chats in Separate Windows:** Off (no check).
- **Keep Chat History:** Forever (you can delete it at any time). How you set the chat-history preference depends on your particular need for security and privacy. If you have particular concerns about where Skype stores chat-history information, refer to the section in Appendix B on where sensitive data is stored for more information.
- **Show Emoticons.** This preference lets you send and receive graphical emotions in text messages. And it translates text emoticons such as a smile or wink ;-) into a small graphical face with a smile or wink gesture. Animated emoticons provide moving graphical icons to depict a greater sense of emotion. The choice to show emoticons is a personal one, and there is no general rule for making a decision about whether to show them.

**Advanced**—This feature provides additional options for Skype application behavior that rarely need to be changed. By default, the preferences are all on (checked). In addition, the Advanced preferences allow network administrators to change the incoming connection port:

- **Port for Incoming Connections:** Set to 0 by default
- **Use Port 80 and 443 As Alternatives for Incoming Connections:** Selected by default

These port settings configure Skype to "listen" for incoming communications from other Skype users—that is, assuming that the data is not blocked by a firewall. Skype does not send outgoing UDP packets from this port. As a result, this port setting does not affect outgoing communications or your ability to connect with the Skype network and other Skype users.

## Pocket PC Preferences Menu Summary

The Skype preferences for Pocket PC are limited compared with the many options available in Microsoft Windows.

**Language**—Do you want Skype to launch in English, traditional Chinese, German, or French? By default, the Skype user interface is set to use English. You can choose another language if you prefer, however. To have the change take effect, you must stop and restart Skype.

**Privacy**—Who do you want to be able to call you? Who do you want to be able to send you IMs? These options are self-evident. Typically, Skype users set them as follows:

- **Allow Calls From:** Contacts
- **Allow Messages (Chat) From:** Anyone

**Prevent Device Standby Mode When Online**—This feature prevents your Pocket PC device from going into standby mode (sleep) while Skype is running. By default, this setting is off (not checked) to conserve battery power. If, however, your Pocket PC device has external power through a USB connection or AC adapter, you may want to turn this option on so that Skype stays connected to the network.

**Echo Cancellation ON**—This feature optimizes the sound quality through enhanced digital signal processing to reduce the effects of audible echoes on a call. This option is important in situations where you are using a built-in microphone and speakers, such that the sound from a speaker re-enters the microphone and causes an echo. In general, this does not happen when you're using earphones, because the sound between the speaker and the microphone is adequately separated. This option is Off by default to prevent your Pocket PC device from working harder than necessary.

## Linux Preferences Menu Summary

**General**—Do you want Skype to launch when you start your computer and log in? When you click a contact, do you want Skype to start a chat or a call? How long do you want Skype to wait before changing your status to unavailable?

- **Check for Updates Automatically** is a great way to be notified and stay up to date with the latest version of Skype.

- **When I Double-Click a Contact** determines whether double-clicking a contact initiates a chat session or a voice call. It's your choice, and it's a personal preference.

- **Show Me 'Away'** and **Show Me As 'Not Available'** provides a mechanism to configure the Skype application to change your online status indicator automatically, depending on how much time has passed since you have interacted with your computer.

- **Browser** sets the default Web browser you want Skype to launch. If you're using the Gnome desktop manager, enter the command-line name for the browser you want to use. If you are using KDE, enter **kfmclient openURL** to launch the Web browser you have configured in your KDE Control Center.

- **Watermarks on Widgets** allows you to turn off any graphical background images or watermarks behind text in Linux widgets, which is especially useful when watermarks interfere with the contrast between the text and its background.

- **Do Not Show Main Window at Start-Up** is a good option to set if your computer is always connected to the Internet. By default, Skype launches when you log in. This preference hides Skype at startup, instead starting it in the background.

- **Main Window Always on Top** forces the Skype application into the foreground, preventing other windows from eclipsing it. If it is important to have quick access to the Skype application, this is a good option to set.

- **Enable Emoticons** lets you send and receive graphical emotions in text messages. And it translates text emoticons such as a smile or wink ;-) into a small graphical face with a smile or wink gesture. The choice to show emoticons is a very personal one, and there is no general rule for whether to enable them.

**Privacy**—Who do you want to be able to call you? Who do you want to be able to send you IMs? Who do you want to be able to call using your SkypeIn number? How long do you want your chat history kept? Although these options are self-evident, typically, Skype users set them as follows:

- **Allow Calls From:** Only people from my Contacts List
- **Allow Chats From:** Anyone
- **Keep Chat History:** Forever (you can delete it at any time). How you set the chat-history preference depends on your particular need for security and privacy. If you have particular concerns about where Skype stores chat-history information, refer to the section in Appendix B on where sensitive data is stored for more information.
- Choose **Remember My Password on This Computer** only if you are the only person who uses the computer or if you have a separate login. Otherwise, other people who use the computer may inadvertently use your Skype account.

**Manage Blocked Users**—This feature allows you to specify Skype Names that you want to block from contacting you under any circumstances.

**Hand/Headset Settings**—This feature provides a graphical user interface for setting the Linux device for calls and ringing. In general, both of these should be set to /dev/dsp.

**Call Alerts**—This feature lets you specify pop-up windows, sounds, and other system behaviors that the Skype application triggers to alert you to the fact that something of interest has happened. The default settings generally are fine, but you can fine-tune them, if you like:

- **When a Contact Calls Me:**
  - **Pop up Window with Call:** Selected by default
  - **Play Ringtone:** Selected by default
  - **Ring PC Speaker:** Off by default but a good option to enable
  - **Automatically Answer Call:** Off by default
  - **Display Notification in System Tray:** Off by default
- **When Someone Not in My Contact List Calls Me:**

NOTE  You will observe the following call alerts only if you have configured privacy options to allow people who are not in your Contacts List to call you.

- **Pop up Window with Call:** Selected by default
- **Play Ringtone:** Selected by default
- **Ring PC Speaker:** Off by default but a good option to enable
- **Automatically Answer Call:** Off by default
- **Display Notification in System Tray:** Off by default

**Chat Alerts**—This feature lets you specify pop-up windows, sounds, and other system behaviors that the Skype application triggers to alert you to the fact that something of interest has happened.

- **When a Contact Sends Me a Chat Message:**
  - **Pop up Chat Window:** Selected by default
  - **Sound an Audio Alert:** Selected by default
  - **Automatically Answer Call:** Off by default
  - **Display Notification in System Tray:** Off by default
- **When Someone Not in My Contact List Sends Me a Message:**

  - **Pop up Chat Window:** Selected by default
  - **Sound an Audio Alert:** Selected by default
  - **Automatically Answer Call:** Off by default
  - **Display Notification in System Tray:** Off by default
  - **Automatically Pop up Incoming Authorization Requests:** Selected by default

**NOTE**    You will observe the call alerts only if you have configured privacy options to allow people who are not in your Contacts List to chat with you.

**Advanced**—This feature provides additional options for Skype application behavior that rarely need to be changed. Advanced preferences allow system and network administrators to change the incoming connection port:

- **Port for Incoming Connections:** Set to 0 by default

- **Use Port 80 and 443 As Alternatives for Incoming Connections:** Selected by default

These port settings configure Skype to "listen" for incoming communications from other Skype users—that is, assuming that the data is not blocked by a firewall. Skype does not send outgoing UDP packets from this port. As a result, this port setting does not affect outgoing communications or your ability to connect with the Skype network and other Skype users.

- **Close Call Tab after Completed Call:** Selected by default
- **Display Technical Call Information:** Off by default. Network administrators, and software and hardware developers may use this option to analyze information about Skype calls.
- **Display On-Line Notifications in the System Tray:** Off by default
- **Set Chat Style:** Set to Skype by default. This really depends on how you prefer to use Skype. Although many Skype users prefer to leave the default setting alone, people who have used the IRC chat system for a long time may prefer to alter how Skype presents chat sessions.

In this chapter,
you learn how to:

Manage your Skype contacts

•

Change your profile and online status

•

Make all types of calls
(including video calls)

•

Communicate effectively with
chat (instant messaging)

•

Participate in conference calls
and multiperson chats

•

Transfer files using
the Skype network

•

Use the Skype application to
enhance your communications

# Using Skype Every Day

This chapter is for anyone who wants to gain a detailed understanding of all of Skype's features and functions. Skype was designed to be simple to use, so it's easy to learn. For those who are already familiar with instant-messaging applications, Skype's operations will seem very straightforward.

## Skype Experience

The experience of using Skype is unique. Because Skype shows you which of your contacts are available and online at any moment, you are always loosely linked to the people in your personal community.

This sense of presence—of knowing who is available and willing to interact—makes communicating infinitely easier. You can "ping" someone with a Skype instant message (IM) to send a brief note, ask a question, or simply say hello. And because instant messaging is less formal and doesn't demand an immediate response, you can interact comfortably over an extended period of time without having to pick up the phone and risk interrupting. When you're ready to talk, you can make a voice call with a touch of a button.

Presence also alters the effects of time and distance. When people in your Skype Contacts List are online and available, you don't have to think of them as being in a particular time zone or locale. And because there is no cost to interact with other Skype users, it doesn't matter where your contacts physically are; they can be in your hometown or in another country thousands of miles away.

With Skype, you have a new opportunity to meet people from all over the world in a way that respects mutual privacy and keeps you in control of how you manage your contacts. You can choose to interact with someone new in chat before allowing them to call you, for example, or block unauthorized users from contacting you at all.

You can also switch from one mode to another as your communication needs shift. You can start in chat and switch to voice. You can talk with someone in the morning and then share IMs for updates throughout the day. You can also interact in different modes simultaneously to do things like send files while talking, drop screen shots directly into chat, or host a conference call while chatting (IMing) in the background with a colleague.

Skype offers a dramatically enhanced communication experience, but it is not foolproof or perfect. Skype will not work if you lose your Internet connection (or your electricity), and there currently is no support for emergency services such as 911 in the United States. You may also experience echoes on the line, jitters, warbling, and other call artifacts if your computer is old, your Internet connection is slow, or your computer is limited by a highly restrictive firewall.

Skype currently may not have all the features of a mature telephone system, but continue to watch for new features and enhancements, as Skype Technologies is upgrading the software and services continually.

# General Features

This section covers the features that are central to understanding and using Skype. These features include Skype contacts, online status icons, user authorizations, privacy management features, and your Personal Profile.

NOTE     You might notice slight differences between what's covered here and the particular version of Skype you are using. Skype Technologies continually adds new features to update the look and feel of the Skype application and Skype Web site. You may also notice differences depending on which operating system you are using, because Skype has been designed to work with many operating platforms.

## Skype Contacts

*Contacts* are people in the Skype network with whom you want to communicate. Your Contacts List is the list of Skype Names in your Skype application that comprise your personal set of contacts.

For instructions on how to add a contact to your Contacts List, please refer to Chapter 4.

### Send a Contact to Another Skype User

You can send a contact from your Contacts List to another Skype user. If your sister joins Skype and wants your cousin's Skype Name, you can send it to her so that she can call your cousin directly.

To send a contact to another Skype user, follow these steps:

1. Choose **Contacts** > **Send Contacts**.

2. Type the Skype Name(s) of the recipient(s).

3. Select the contacts you wish to send; click **Add**; and then click **Send** (see Figure 5-1).

Alternatively, you can right-click a contact and select **Send Contacts** from the context menu. (Mac users: Control-click and select **Send Contacts** from the context menu.)

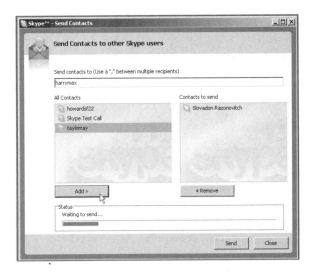

**Figure 5–1** Send contacts

## Invite Someone to Use Skype

To invite someone you know to join the Skype network (so he can be added to your Contacts List), choose **Tools** > **Share Skype with a Friend**. (Mac users: Choose **Contacts** > **Share Skype with a Friend**.) This will launch a Web page where you can send an e-mail invitation to multiple people with a link to download Skype.

## Delete a Contact

To remove a contact from your Contacts List, right-click the Skype Name, and select **Remove from Contacts** from the context menu. (Mac users: Control-click, and select **Remove from Contacts** from the context menu.) Deleting a contact only removes the contact's information from your Contacts List; it does not prevent someone from contacting you.

## Block a Contact

Blocking a contact prevents someone from contacting you. To block a contact, right-click the Skype Name, and select **Block User** from the context menu. (Mac users: Control-click the Skype Name, and select **Block** from the context menu.) Skype users who have been blocked will not be able to contact you in any way.

To unblock a user, choose **Tools** > **Options** > **Privacy**, and click the **Manage Blocked Users** link. Select the Skype Name of the person you want to unblock, and click **Unblock**. (Mac users: Choose **Contacts** > **Manage Blocked Users**. Select the Skype Name of the person you want to unblock, and click **Unblock User.**)

NOTE    You can also set your privacy settings to manage who is allowed to contact you. See the "Privacy Features" section later in this chapter for more information.

## Contact Groups

Skype for Windows gives you the option of putting your contacts into groups so you can see your contacts organized in ways that make sense to you (such as Work, Friends, or Family). You have the option of creating your own groups or using Skype's predefined categories.

Having contact groups helps organize your Contacts List and makes it easy to start a regular conference call or multiperson chat.

NOTE    The contact-group feature currently is available only for Skype for Windows. Check the Skype Web site for ongoing updates to Skype for other operating systems.

### Create a Group

To create your own Skype group, follow these steps:

1. Choose **View** > **Show Contact Groups**.

2. Click the **+** icon in the group box to create a new group.

3. Enter a title for the group, and press **Enter**.

   You will see the group in the list.

4. To add contacts to the group, select a Skype Name from your Contacts List, and drag it to a group in the list.

   You will see a number to the right of the group name, indicating how many contacts are in that group (see Figure 5-2).

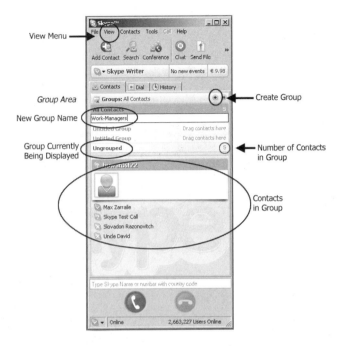

**Figure 5-2**   Create a new group

## Display a Group

To view a Skype group, follow these steps:

1. Choose **View** > **Show Contact Groups**.

2. If the group list is not expanded, click the bottom of the group box to expand the list.

3. Double-click the group name to display the group.

   The contacts in the group will be displayed in your Contacts List in the Skype main window.

   Alternatively, you can choose **View** > **Show Contact Groups**; click the **>>** icon; and select a group from the list (see Figure 5-3).

## Remove a Contact from a Group

To remove a contact from a particular group, follow these steps:

1. Display the group.

2. Right-click the Skype Name of the person you want to remove from the Contacts List, and select **Remove from *Group Name*** from the context menu.

   For ***Group Name***, substitute the name of the actual group.

**Figure 5–3** Display a group

## Delete a Group

To delete a group, follow these steps:

1. Display the group.

2. Right-click the group name, and select **Remove Group** from the context menu.

## Display All Contacts (Ungrouped)

To view all your contacts (ungrouped), open the View menu, and deselect Show Contact Groups (see Figure 5-4).

**Figure 5–4**    Display all contacts

## Display a Skype Predefined Group

To view a predefined group, follow these steps:

1. Choose **View** > **Show Contact Groups**.

2. Click the **>>** icon.

3. Select **Predefined Groups**.

4. Select the group you want to display.

    The contacts in the group will be displayed in your Contacts List in the Skype main window (see Figure 5-5).

## Make a Conference Call, Start a Multiperson Chat, or Send a File to a Group

To make a call, start a chat, or send a file to one of your groups, right-click the group, and select the action you want to take from the context menu (see Figure 5-6).

**Figure 5–5**
Display a predefined group

**Figure 5–6**
Make a conference
call to a group

## Online Status Icons

Each contact in your Contacts List will have an icon next to the name that indicates online status. This status tells you whether the contact is logged into Skype and available for communicating. Table 5-1 lists the Skype online statuses.

Your own online status is displayed at the bottom of your Skype main window. To change your online status at any given moment, click your **Status** icon, and select a new status from the drop-down menu, or choose **File** > **Change Online Status**, and select a new status. (Mac users: Choose **Account** > **Change Status**.)

To protect your privacy, Skype shows your online status only to those users whom you have explicitly authorized to see this information. See the "Authorizations and Online Status" section later in this chapter for more information.

**Table 5–1**   Online Status Options

| Status | Icon | Description |
|--------|------|-------------|
| Online | | User is logged into Skype and is available for contact. (This is the Skype default.) |
| SkypeMe | | User is logged into Skype, is available for contact, and wants to be contacted by anyone in the Skype network. This is a good way for users in a local area to find one another, because the Skype search tool has a special search for people in SkypeMe mode. (In SkypeMe mode, the user's privacy settings are disabled so that anyone can initiate contact. These settings are restored as soon as the user changes to any other status.) |
| Away | | User is logged into Skype but is not currently using it. Default is set to 20 minutes. To change this time, go to your Skype preferences. |
| Not Available | | User is logged into Skype but is not currently using it. Default is set to 60 minutes. To change this time, go to your Skype preferences. |
| Do Not Disturb | | User is logged in but does not want to be disturbed. Do Not Disturb status disables the pop-up feature for new chat messages. New messages are stored for later viewing in the Missed Events area. |
| Invisible | | User will appear offline to other Skype users but is actually logged into Skype. |
| Not Yet Authorized | | User has not yet granted you permission to see her contact details and online status. |
| Offline | | User is not logged into Skype (or has chosen to be invisible). Please note: An offline user can go back online simply by changing the status. Therefore, if you leave your computer (especially in a public place), it is important that you actually log off Skype so that no one can use your Skype account on your computer without your knowledge. To log off, choose **File** > **Log Off**. |
| Offline (Call Forwarding Activated) | | User is offline and has activated call forwarding. |
| SkypeOut | | User is a SkypeOut contact. |

125

NOTE     When you change your online status, Skype will maintain this status until you change it again. If you change your status to SkypeMe, for example, when you log off and log back on again, your Skype will once again show your status as Skype Me.

## Authorizations and Online Status

When you add a contact to your Contacts List, Skype will automatically ask you whether you want to share your contact details with that person. When you share your contact details with someone, you *authorize* him to see your full name, your profile information, and your online status.

To send your contact details, fill out the Send Contact Details screen (which you display by clicking **Add Selected Contact**), and select the option you want, as shown in Figure 5-7.

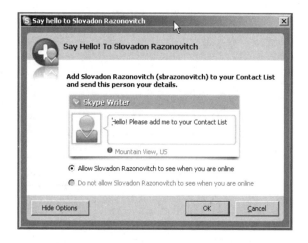

**Figure 5–7**   Send contact details (Microsoft Windows)

The contact will be notified that he has been added to your Contacts List and will, in turn, be asked whether he wants to share his contact details with you (see Figure 5-8).

A contact's online status will be displayed as a question mark (?) until you are authorized to see it. You will not be able to see a contact's online status unless he explicitly authorizes you to see his contact details.

To ask someone to resend contact details, right-click the Skype Name, and select **Request Contact Details** from the context menu. (Mac users: Control-click the Skype Name, and select **Request Authorization** from the context menu.)

**Figure 5–8**   Respond to request

## Privacy Features

In addition to being able to choose who can see your online status, you
have the option of specifying who can contact you (see Figure 5-9).

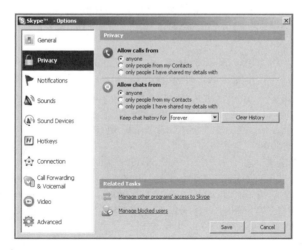

**Figure 5–9**   Privacy options

You can choose to allow calls from:

- Anyone in the Skype network
- Only people on your Contacts List
- Only people you have authorized to see your online status

You also have the option of allowing IMs from:

- Anyone in the Skype network
- Only people on your Contacts List
- Only people you have authorized to see your online status

These two options are set separately, so you can configure your Skype to suit your individual preferences and needs. Choose **Tools** > **Options** > **Privacy** to configure these settings. (Mac users: Choose **Skype** > **Preferences** > **Privacy**.)

Again, Skype allows you to block a user completely from communicating with you, if necessary. For more information, see the "Block a Contact" section earlier in this chapter.

## Your Personal Profile

Your Personal Profile is optional information that you choose to share with other Skype users so that they can locate you by using this information (see Figure 5-10). Please note that your Personal Profile data is stored in the shared Skype peer-to-peer (P2P) network on the Internet. You can always delete or change your Personal Profile information by choosing **File** > **Edit My Profile**. (Mac users: Choose **Account** > **My Profile**.)

### Add, Edit, or Delete the Text in Your Profile

To update your profile, simply change the information in your profile, and save it. To delete information in your profile, simply overwrite the existing information with blank spaces, and save it. Your profile is reestablished every time you log in and may disappear from the network if you don't log in for a long time.

Remember, your e-mail address is never displayed for others to see. If someone already knows your e-mail address, however, she can use it to search for you in the Skype network. Skype Technologies will use your e-mail address to send you a new password (if you forget it) and to communicate with you about your account.

For this reason, it is strongly recommended that you use a valid e-mail address in your Skype profile. If you do not put a valid e-mail address in your profile, and you forget your password, there is no way to get a new password. You will have to abandon your Skype Name and create a new account.

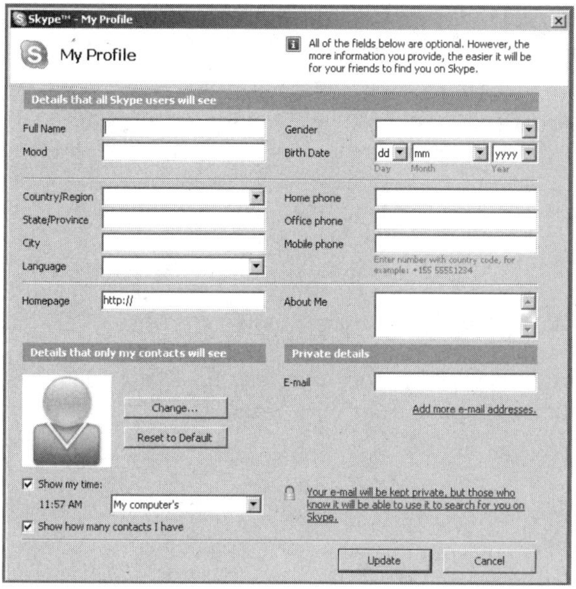

**Figure 5–10**   Edit your profile

You can use your Personal Profile to present a public ''persona'' based on information you share about your life, such as where you live or your interests, profession, expertise, or aspects of your personality. Other Skype users can use this information to find you. And depending on the type of information you include, it can also provide the starting point for an interesting conversation. If you want to have multiple personas, you need to create a separate Skype account for each persona.

Although you can have multiple Skype Names (with unique Personal Profiles), you will not be able to use the same credit card to purchase services such as SkypeOut across multiple accounts. You will need to use a separate credit card for each Skype Name. This is a fraud-protection measure.

## Add a Picture to Your Profile

You have the option of selecting a picture or uploading a bitmap or .JPEG file from your files. This picture is what callers will see when they Skype you.

To select a picture from the list, follow these steps:

1. In the My Profile screen, click the **Change** button.

2. Select a picture from the list, and click **OK**.

   (Mac users: Click **Set** and then click **Update** to update your profile.)

   Alternatively, you can click **Get New Pictures** to buy a photo from the Skype Web site.

To upload a personal image from your files, follow these steps:

1. In the My Profile screen, click the **Change** button.

2. Click **Browse** to select a photo of your own.

3. Select the folder on your computer that holds your photo; click the name of the photo; and click **Open**.

   You should see the photo in the list.

4. Select the photo, and click **OK**.

## Change Password

To change your password, follow these steps:

1. Choose **File** > **My Skype Account** > **Change Password**.

   (Mac users: Choose **Account** > **Change Password**.)

2. Enter your old password; enter your new password; and confirm your new password by reentering it.

3. Click **Apply**.

## Change Skype into Another Language

The Skype application was developed in the English language, but you can choose another language, if you want. To change the language, choose **Tools** > **Select Languages**, and select your preferred language from the list. For instructions on how to edit the Skype user interfaces into a language that is not yet represented, see Appendix C.

If you call the **echo123** answering service after changing the Skype language, you will hear the prompts in the language you have selected. The **echo123** answering service is also available in Chinese, Mandarin, Taiwanese dialect (echo-chinese), and Japanese (soundtestjapanese).

## Upload a Ringtone

You can buy a ringtone from the Skype Web site or upload a sound file of your own. To upload a file of your own, choose **Tools** > **Options** > **Sounds**.

Click the middle folder icon; select a .wav file from your collection; and click **Open**. Then click **Save** to save your changes. (Mac users: Choose **Skype** > **Preferences** > **Events**.)

## Skype Toolbars (Optional)

The Skype toolbar for Internet Explorer, Mozilla Firefox, and Microsoft Outlook is an optional feature that you can download from the Skype Web site. The Skype toolbar allows you to launch various Skype functions from your browser or Outlook without having to open a Skype window. Specifically, you can see which of your contacts are online and make calls or start chats directly from the toolbar. It also includes a link for you to check your Skype account balances or go directly to the Skype Web site (see Figure 5-11).

**Figure 5–11**   Skype toolbar for Internet Explorer

If you open a Web page that has phone numbers on it, the Skype toolbar automatically converts the phone numbers to SkypeOut links so you can call a number, assuming that you have sufficient SkypeOut credit. Simply click the link to be connected immediately. If you open a Web page that has Skype Names on it, you can call, chat, or add contacts to your Contacts List quickly and easily.

The Skype toolbar also contains a text box for searching using Google or Yahoo!, so you do not have to install a search engine toolbar in addition to the Skype toolbar. For instructions on how to install the Skype toolbar, see Chapter 3.

## Skype Widget for Mac OS X

For Mac users, Skype offers a widget for the Mac OS X Dashboard that lets you dial SkypeOut calls, look up country codes, and check calling rates. To download the widget, go to the **Downloads** section of the Skype Web site.

# Voice Calls

The Skype application is easy to use and works in the same way across a variety of activities. With Skype, you typically *select* a contact (or contacts) and then *do* something (make a call, start a conference call, start a video call, send an IM, or transfer a file). You have the choice of clicking an icon or selecting an option from a menu to start an activity.

This section covers how to use Skype for voice calling. It includes how to make and receive calls, start a conference call, make and receive calls from landline and cell phones (SkypeOut and SkypeIn), view your call history, and forward your Skype calls to a landline or cell phone.

## Make a Call

There are four ways to make a call using Skype:

- Select a Skype Name in your Contacts List, and click the big green **Call** button in the bottom-left portion of the Skype main window (see Figure 5-12). This assumes that you have already added a Skype Name to your Contacts List.

**Figure 5–12**   Contact with Call button

- Double-click a Skype Name in your Contacts List (if you have set your Skype preferences to initiate a call versus an IM). If your Skype preferences are set to start a call when you double-click, Skype will start the call. Otherwise, a chat window opens, and you will need to click the big green **Call** button to start a call.

To set this preference, choose **Tools** > **Options** > **General**. (Mac users: Choose **Skype** > **Preferences** > **General**.) For more information on setting preferences, refer to Chapter 4.

- Right-click a Skype Name, and choose **Start Call** from the context menu (see Figure 5-13). (Mac users: Control-click the Skype Name, and choose **Call** from the context menu.) This assumes that you have already added the Skype Name to your Contacts List or have identified a contact by using the Search function.

**Figure 5-13** Contact with Call menu

- Type a conventional phone number (in the appropriate Skype format) in the text box in the bottom portion of the Skype main window, and click the big green **Call** button to use SkypeOut to make a call to a landline or cell phone. For more information on how to use SkypeOut, see the "Call a Landline or Cell Phone (Use SkypeOut)" section later in this chapter.

## Make a Conference Call

You can use Skype to host a conference call with up to four other people (for a total of five, including yourself). The person who initiates a conference call is considered to be the host, and the host is the only person who can add new participants to a call.

NOTE    Because Skype calls use the Skype P2P network, it is best that the conference host have a modern computer and a fast connection to the Internet.

There are three ways to begin a conference call:

- Click the **Conference** icon; select up to four Skype Names; click **Add** to add the names to the conference call; and then click **Start**.

- Choose **Tools** > **Create a Conference Call**. (Mac users: Choose **Call** > **Start a Conference Call**.) Select up to four names; click **Add** to add the names to the conference call; and then click **Start**.

- Select up to four participants from your Contacts List by holding down the Ctrl key and clicking the individual Skype Names. (Mac users: Hold down the Command key to select participants.) Then click the big green **Call** button to initiate calling.

Your conference will start when the participants accept the call.

You can also add people who are not on the Skype network to a conference call. Type the phone number you want to add in the text box in the appropriate Skype format (or select the SkypeOut contact in your Contacts List), and click the **Conference** icon.

When adding a SkypeOut contact to a conference call, you must have sufficient SkypeOut credit for the duration of the call for each person you are calling. For more information about SkypeOut, see the "Call a Landline or Cell Phone (Use SkypeOut)" section later in this chapter.

When you add SkypeOut contacts to a conference call, each call will be charged separately and will appear on your account overview as a separate call. There is no extra charge for SkypeOut conference calling. You simply pay for the time used for each connection. If you have less than 1 minute of SkypeOut credit remaining for any of the calls, Skype will drop the call from the conference. The conference will continue with the remaining users.

Skype users running Linux and Pocket PC can participate in conference calls but currently cannot host them.

## Add Participants to a Live Conference Call

As the host, if you are already on a conference call and you want to add another participant to the discussion, follow these steps:

1. In your Contacts List, select the Skype Name of the person you want to add.

2. Click the **Conference** icon.

   Alternatively, you can right-click the Skype Name and select **Invite to Conference** from the context menu (see Figure 5-14).

(Mac users: Control-click the Skype Name, and select **Add to Conference** from the context menu.)

You can add participants to a conference call up to the five-person maximum limit.

**Figure 5–14** Invite to conference

## Receive a Call

When someone calls you, you will hear a ring, and a message will pop up notifying you of the call. (Mac users: The Skype icon will bounce in the Dock if your Skype preferences are set to do this.)

You can choose to accept the call by clicking the big green **Call** button or to reject the call by clicking the big red **Hang Up** button (see Figure 5-15). When you accept the call, and the call connects, you will see a timestamp with the duration of the call. This timestamp signals that a call has started (see Figure 5-16).

To change the way you are notified of a call, choose **Tools** > **Options** > **Notifications** to change the settings. (Mac users: Choose **Skype** > **Preferences** > **Events**.)

To change the sounds you hear, choose **Tools** > **Options** > **Sounds**. You can download special tones or reset the sounds to the Skype defaults. (Mac users: Choose **Skype** > **Preferences** > **Events**.)

**Figure 5–15**   Call and Hang Up buttons

**Figure 5–16**   Call accepted

If you are using a headset, and you want your computer speakers to ring when you receive a call, choose **Tools** > **Options** > **Sound Devices**, and check the **Ring PC Speaker** checkbox.

## Adjust the Volume of a Call

To adjust the volume of your microphone, speakers, or headset, use the sound Control Panel for your operating system. To open this Control Panel, choose **Start** > **Settings** > **Control Panel** > **Sounds and Audio Devices**. (Mac OS X users: Choose **Apple** > **System Preferences** > **Sound**.)

## End a Call

You can end a call at any time by clicking the big red **Hang Up** button in the bottom-right portion of the Skype main window. You can also end the call from the **Call** menu.

## Call a Landline or Cell Phone (Use SkypeOut)

To call someone outside the Skype network (someone using a landline or cell phone), you need to buy SkypeOut credit to allow Skype to connect your call using the traditional telephone network. SkypeOut credit rates vary depending on the country you are calling, but the rates start at approximately 2 cents per minute.

For current SkypeOut pricing, go to the **My Account** section of the Skype main window, and click the **SkypeOut** link. You will be taken to the Skype Web site and will be asked to log in to your account page with your Skype Name and password. Alternatively, you can go to the Skype Web site by typing **www.skype.com** in the address bar of your Web browser.

Your SkypeOut credit remains active for 180 days after your last successfully connected SkypeOut phone call. To use SkypeOut, you need to have a positive credit balance (at least enough credit to make a 1-minute call to the country you want to call).

### Buy SkypeOut Credit

To buy SkypeOut credit, follow these steps:

1. In the **My Account** section of the Skype main window, click the **SkypeOut** link.

   This will take you to the Skype Web site, where you will need to log in with your Skype Name and password.

2. When you are logged in, check the rates for the country you want to call by clicking the **SkypeOut Calling Rates** link.

   This rate sheet lists calling rates for nearly every country. Select the currency type for your home country to see these rates in your currency.

3. Click the **Buy Skype Credit** link.

4. Select the amount of credit you want by clicking the **Buy This** button.

5. Fill out your address information (if you want to save this information for later use, you can give it a name), or click **Use This Address Only Once**.

6. Select a payment method, and click **Continue**.

7. Fill out your payment details.

   Skype protects against credit-card fraud by limiting each Skype Name to one credit card. To buy SkypeOut credit for a different Skype Name, you will need to use a different credit card.

NOTE   If you live in the United States, the Skype form separates the house number from the street address, so you may need to re-enter your house number.

8. Click **Submit** to place your order.

   You will receive an e-mail when your SkypeOut credits have been activated, and you will see your current SkypeOut balance displayed in the **My Accounts** section of the Skype main window (see Figure 5-17).

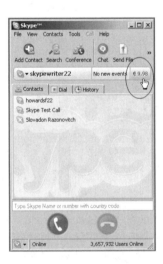

**Figure 5–17**   SkypeOut credit balance

## Buy SkypeOut Credit for a Group

You can also buy SkypeOut credit to be used by a group of people (such as family members or work teams). This feature allows a group administrator to buy SkypeOut credit (as well as SkypeIn numbers and voicemail subscriptions) to manage the billing centrally. To administer a Skype group, go to www.skype.com/products/skypegroups/.

## Make a SkypeOut Call

When you have SkypeOut credit in your account, you can use the dial pad to make a call outside the Skype network. You can also type the number in the text box in the bottom portion of the Skype main window.

To make a SkypeOut call, enter a plus sign (**+**) and the number in a specific format; then click the big green **Call** button. The specific format for SkypeOut is + *country code area code number.*

Here is an example:

+16505551212

The country code is 1; the area code is 650; and the number is 5551212.

> NOTE   The country code is always included, even if you are calling the same country in which you reside. If you do not know the country code you need to dial, you can use the Skype Dialing Wizard at www.skype.com/products/skypeout/rates/dialing.html.

You can also get to the Dialing Wizard by using the Help menu. Choose **Help** > **Help**; click **Knowledgebase**; type **Dialing Wizard** in the search box; and click **Search Knowledgebase**. Then click the **Where Can I Get the Country Codes for Dialing?** link in the search results.

> WARNING   Skype cannot be used for dialing emergency services anywhere in the world, such as 911 in the United States. If you try to call 911 using Skype, you will not be connected.

## Receive a Call from a Landline or Cell Phone (Use SkypeIn)

A SkypeIn number is a telephone number that you purchase so that people outside the Skype network can call a regular telephone number and reach you on Skype. When you purchase a SkypeIn number, you also receive a voicemail subscription at no extra cost, so callers can leave you a message if you are not available.

SkypeIn numbers currently are available in Denmark, Estonia, Finland, France, Germany, Hong Kong SAR, Poland, Sweden, Switzerland, the United Kingdom, and the United States. Be sure to check the Skype Web site, as new areas are being added continually.

Skype allows you to buy up to ten SkypeIn numbers (in a variety of states and countries) per Skype Name. This means that if you have friends in different countries or states, you can purchase a number in a country or area code that is convenient and cost effective for them. That way, they can call you using a number that is local to them (avoiding long-distance charges), and you will receive the call on Skype.

When someone calls you using a SkypeIn number, she will hear a normal telephone ring and will not know that she is calling you on Skype. If you are logged into Skype, you will hear the ring, and a pop-up message will notify you of the call. If you aren't available to take the call (or if you reject the call), the caller will go to voicemail automatically. If you are not logged into Skype, the caller will hear the phone ringing and then go directly to voicemail (unless you have call forwarding activated).

## Buy a SkypeIn Number (with Voicemail)

To purchase a SkypeIn number (and free voicemail subscription), go to the **My Account** section of the Skype main window, and click the **SkypeIn** link. You will be taken to the Skype Web site and will be asked to log in to your account page with your Skype Name and password.

When you are logged in, follow these steps:

1. Click the **Buy SkypeIn Number** link.

2. Select a country where you want callers to be able to reach you and an area code (if appropriate).

3. Select the number you prefer.

   Write this down.

4. Click the subscription option you want—3 months or 12 months—and then click the **Buy Selected Number** button.

5. Fill out your address information (if you want to save this information for later use, you can give it a name), or click **Use This Address Only Once**.

6. Select a payment method, and click **Continue**.

7. Fill out your payment details.

8. Click **Submit** to place your order.

   You will receive an e-mail when your SkypeIn number is activated.

**NOTE** If you live in the United States, the online form separates the house number from the street address, so you may need to re-enter your house number.

To see your SkypeIn number, follow these steps:

1. In the **My Account** section of the Skype main window, click the **SkypeIn** link. You will be taken to the Skype Web site and will be asked to log in to your account page with your Skype Name and password.

2. When you are logged in, click **My Account**. You will see a summary of the services you have, with expiration dates (see Figure 5-18).

**Figure 5–18** My Account page

**NOTE**     For security purposes, Skype Technologies allows only one credit card per Skype Name. If you have multiple Skype Names and want to purchase services for these accounts, you will need to use multiple credit cards. This is a fraud-protection measure.

## Buy SkypeIn Numbers for a Group

You can also buy SkypeIn numbers to be used by a group of people (such as family members or work teams). This feature allows a group administrator to buy SkypeIn numbers (and SkypeOut credit, as well as voicemail subscriptions) to manage the billing centrally. To administer a Skype group, go to www.skype.com/products/skypegroups/.

## View and Clear Call History

Your call history is easily accessible via the **History** tab (or the **Call List** tab in all of the operating systems other than Windows). You can view all calls, missed calls, received calls, and sent calls, and you can sort calls by contact. You can also listen to your voicemails from the **History** tab (see Figure 5-19).

**Figure 5–19**   History tab

To initiate a call, chat, or file transfer directly from the **History** tab, right-click a Skype Name in the list, and select an option from the context menu. (Mac users: In the **Call List** tab, Control-click a Skype Name, and select an option from the context menu.) To listen to a voicemail message, click the **Voicemail** icon.

To clear your call history, choose **Tools** > **Clear History**. (Mac users: Choose **Call** > **Clear Call List**.)You can delete your call history from the Skype application on your computer, but you cannot delete your SkypeOut call history in the **My Account** section of the Skype Web site.

## Forward Calls from Skype

You can elect to have your Skype calls redirected to a cell or landline phone so that you can receive calls even if you are not on Skype. This is helpful when you need to be away from your computer or PDA but still have important calls you want to answer.

When you use call forwarding, your incoming Skype calls are relayed to up to three different numbers that you designate, even if your computer is off. Because these calls travel outside Skype's network, a forwarded call is charged just like a SkypeOut call.

When call forwarding is activated, and your Skype is open, your Skype will ring, and the call will roll to your forwarded number(s). If your computer is off or Skype is closed, the call will forward without ringing.

You can also forward your calls from one Skype Name to another. Because this forwarding is within the Skype network, there is no charge for this forwarding. Please note, however, that callers will get a message saying that the "caller is offline" if you are not logged in to the destination Skype Name.

## Activate Call Forwarding

To forward your calls to one or more phone numbers, follow these steps:

1. Choose **Tools** > **Options** > **Call Forwarding & Voicemail**.

   (Mac users: Choose **Skype** > **Preferences** > **Calls**.)

2. Check the **Forward Calls When I'm Not on Skype** checkbox, and enter a phone number (see Figure 5-20).

   (Mac users: Check the **Forward Unanswered Calls To** checkbox, and enter a phone number.)

   The phone number must be in the specific Skype format: + *country code area code number.* An example is +16505551212. The country code is 1; the area code is 650; and the number is 5551212.

   You can forward to up to three numbers. Just enter the numbers in the designated boxes.

3. Click **Save**.

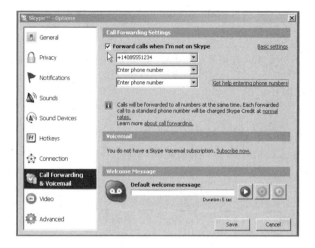

**Figure 5–20** Call forwarding

## Deactivate Call Forwarding

To stop forwarding your calls to other phone numbers, follow these steps:

1. Choose **Tools** > **Options** > **Call Forwarding & Voicemail**.

   (Mac users: Choose **Skype** > **Preferences** > **Calls**.)

2. Uncheck the **Forward Calls When I'm Not on Skype** checkbox.

   (Mac users: Uncheck the **Forward Unanswered Calls To** checkbox.)

3. Click **Save**.

> NOTE   You need to be using at least Skype version 1.4 to activate call forwarding. Also, if you are forwarding to another Skype Name, the Skype Name to which you are forwarding calls must be online. Some Skype users also may experience problems with their call forwarding if their privacy settings are set to allow only people on their Contacts List to contact them.

# Voicemail

Skype voicemail allows callers to leave you a message if you are not available, are offline, or reject a call. A unique feature of Skype voicemail is that it acts like a voice *messaging* service. You can leave voice messages for other Skype users without having to ring their Skype, and as long as you have a voicemail subscription, you can leave voice messages for people who don't have voicemail.

When you have a voicemail subscription, other Skype users will see a **Voicemail** icon next to your Skype Name (see Figure 5-21), and callers can leave you a voicemail message even if you are not online. The next time you log into Skype, you will be notified of the message.

**Figure 5–21**   Voicemail icon

You can choose to have callers automatically transferred to voicemail when you are on another call and specify how long a caller should hear a ring you before being sent to voicemail. To set your voicemail preferences, choose **Tools > Options > Call Forwarding & Voicemail**. (Mac users: Choose **Skype > Preferences > Calls**.)

NOTE     For another Skype user to leave you a message, your caller must be using a recent version of Skype. You can determine whether you need to upgrade your version of Skype by choosing **Help > Check for Update**. (Mac users: Choose **Skype > Check for Update**.) Alternatively, point your Web browser to www.skype.com/downloads, and install the new version of Skype on top of the version you have.

## Listen to a Voicemail

When you have a new voicemail, the **Events** section of the Skype main window will display a red flag and a text message to alert you to the voicemail. You can click the **Events** section or go to the **History** tab to listen to the voicemail message.

- To play a message, click the round green **Play** button.
- To delete a message from your queue, click the **Trash Can** icon.

As soon as you listen to a voicemail message, it is transferred from the Skype servers to your computer and stored locally on your computer as an unencrypted file with a .DAT extension. Unplayed voicemail messages are stored on the Skype servers for 60 days before being deleted.

## Send a Voice Message

To send a voice message to another Skype user without ringing Skype, right-click the Skype Name, and select **Send Voicemail** from the context menu. (Mac users: Control-click the Skype Name, and select **Send Voicemail** from the context menu.) You will hear a message telling you that the caller is unavailable. Speak after the beep.

## Record a Voicemail Greeting

You can choose to have your voicemail use a standard greeting to greet callers when you are not available, or you can record your own personalized greeting.

To record a personalized greeting, follow these steps:

1. Choose **Tools** > **Options** > **Call Forwarding & Voicemail** (see Figure 5-22).

   (Mac users: Choose **Skype** > **Preferences** > **Calls**.)

2. Click the red record button in the middle, and record your message.

3. Click the green **Play** button to hear your message.

4. Click **Save** to save the recording.

If you want to restore the greeting to the standardized greeting, click the red loop arrow button, and click **Save**.

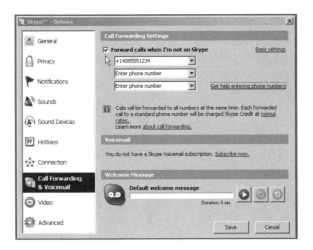

**Figure 5–22**   Voicemail options

# Video Calls

If the person calling you has a Webcam, you can receive the video call using Skype. If you have a Webcam, you can use Skype to make a video call.

NOTE    Video calling currently is available only in Skype for Microsoft Windows. Check the Skype Web site for ongoing updates to Skype for other operating systems.

## Receive a Video Call

Even if *you* don't have a Webcam, you can receive a video call. To receive a video call, follow these steps:

1. Answer a Skype call.

2. When you see **Receive Skype Video?** click **OK**.

    A video screen will be displayed in the center of your Skype main window.

3. To enlarge the video, right-click the video window, and select **View > Full Screen Video** from the context menu (see Figure 5-23).

4. To return the video picture to the Call tab, click **Video on Call Tab**.

**Figure 5–23** Enlarge video image

## Make a Video Call

When you log in, Skype will detect the presence of a Webcam automatically and allow you to adjust your Webcam settings. Be sure that the device is working properly before making a call. Click **Webcam Settings**, and adjust the settings as needed (see Figure 5-24).

You may also want to view the Skype video options to make sure that your video preferences are set properly. Click **Video** in the Skype Options window to set your video-calling preferences (see Figure 5-25).

NOTE    If you check the Start My Video Automatically checkbox as one of your video preferences, your Skype will start transmitting video as soon the person you are calling answers. If you uncheck this checkbox, you will have the option of starting your video transmission at any time during the call.

**Figure 5–24** Webcam test

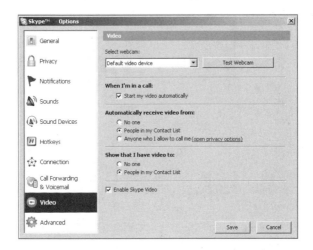

**Figure 5–25** Video options

To make a video call, follow these steps:

1.  Make sure that your Webcam is working properly.

2.  Select a Skype Name from your Contacts List, and click the big green **Call** button.

If the person you are calling is transmitting video, you will see it in the center of your Skype main window.

3. Click **Start My Video** to begin your video transmission, if it has not started automatically (see Figure 5-26).

**Figure 5–26**   Start video

4. To enlarge the video image, right-click the video window, and select **View** > **Full Screen Video** from the context menu (see Figure 5-27).

To reduce the video image, click **Video on Call Tab**.

5. To stop your video transmission, click **Stop My Video**.

6. To end the call, simply hang up.

**Figure 5-27**   Enlarge video image

# Chat (Instant Messaging)

Starting a chat (or sending an IM) using Skype is similar to making a call with Skype. You typically *select* a contact (or contacts) and then *do* something (send an IM, start a multiperson chat, or send a file while chatting).

This section covers how to use Skype for chat/instant messaging. It includes how to send and reply to an IM, start a multiperson chat, add a person to an existing chat, call and transfer files while chatting, bookmark a chat, and view and clear chat history.

## Send an IM (Start a Chat Session)

There are three ways to send an IM and start a chat:

- Select a Skype Name in your Contacts List, and click the **Chat** icon. (Mac users: Select a Skype Name, and click the **Send IM** icon.)

- Right-click a Skype Name in your Contacts List or in the search results, and choose **Start Chat** from the context menu. (Mac users: Control-click the Skype Name, and choose **Send Instant Message** from the context menu.)

• Double-click the Skype Name in your Contacts List.

Double-clicking a Skype Name will start a chat if you have set your Skype preferences to do this. To set this preference, choose **Tools** > **Options** > **General**. (Mac users: Choose **Skype** > **Preferences** > **General**.)

If this is the first time you are chatting with someone, you will see an empty chat history and the name of your chat partner in the right corner. Type your message in the smaller text-input box at the bottom of the Chat Window.

When you press **Enter** on your keyboard, the message is sent, and you will see it displayed in the chat-history. By default, Skype is configured to send a message when you press Enter.

To change this setting, choose **Tools** > **Options** > **Hot Keys**. If you change this setting, you will need to click the carriage-return icon in the chat window to send a message (or press Alt+S).

When the person receiving your message responds, you will see the response in the chat-history (see Figure 5-28).

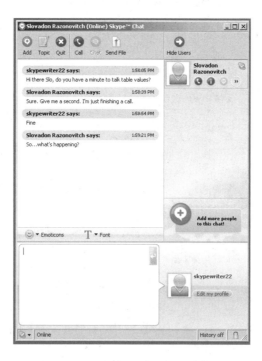

**Figure 5–28**   Chat window

If this is not the first time you are chatting with someone, you will see a record of the preceding chat. To see complete chat histories and clear them, see the "View and Clear Chat History" section later in this chapter.

The chat will stay active (and you will be notified of any new messages) if you move the chat window out of view, minimize the chat window, or close it.

To exit a chat permanently, click the **Quit** icon on the toolbar (see Figure 5-29). Clicking the **Quit** icon will end your participation in the chat, and you will not be notified of any new messages.

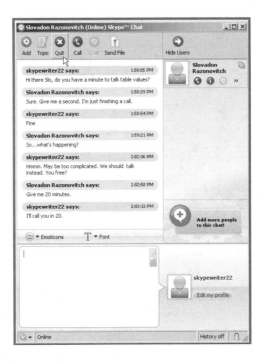

**Figure 5–29**   Quit chat

By default, Skype pops open a new window for each new chat session. If you are a heavy chat user—that is, you chat frequently or with many people simultaneously—you may want to set your preferences to disable the pop-up-window feature. To reset this preference, choose **Tools > Options > Advanced**. For details on setting notification and advanced preferences, see Chapter 4.

## Start a Multiperson Chat

You can also start a chat involving up to 50 people. To start a multiperson chat, follow these steps:

1. Select multiple Skype Names from your Contacts List by holding down the Ctrl key and clicking each Skype Name.

   (Mac users: Hold down the Command key and click each Skype Name.)

2. Click the **Chat** icon in the Skype main window.

   You will see a standard chat window with the participants displayed on the right side (see Figure 5-30).

   Again, the chat stays active (and you will be notified of any new messages) if you move the chat window out of view, minimize the chat window, or close it.

**Figure 5–30**   Starting multiperson chat

3. To exit a chat permanently, click the **Quit** icon on the toolbar.

   Clicking the **Quit** icon will end your participation in the chat, and you will *not* be notified of any new messages.

## Add a Participant to a Live Chat

To add another participant to an ongoing chat, follow these steps:

1. Click the **Add More People to This Chat!** icon in the bottom-right portion of the chat window (see Figure 5-31).

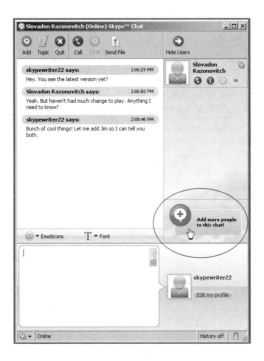

**Figure 5–31**   Add users to existing chat

2. Select a contact; click **Add**; and then click **OK**.

   You will see the new user displayed on the right side of the chat window.

NOTE    Each participant in a multiperson chat must be using the latest version of Skype. You can determine whether you need to upgrade your version of Skype by choosing **Help** > **Check for Update**. (Mac users: Choose **Skype** > **Check for Update**.) Alternatively, point your Web browser to www.skype.com/downloads, and install the new version of Skype on top of the version you have.

## Transfer a File While Chatting

If you want to send a file to someone (or a group of people) you are chatting with, you can drag and drop the file directly into the chat window. Alternatively, you can click the **Send File** icon (see Figure 5-32); select a file; and click **Open**. The transfer process will start, but the recipient will need to accept the file before the file can be transferred.

**Figure 5-32**   Transferring files while chatting

NOTE        Drag and drop is well supported in Skype. You can drag and drop a file into a chat session or to a Skype Name (to transfer a file), or drag and drop a Skype Name among chats (to add someone to a chat).

## Make a Call While Chatting

To call the person with whom you are chatting, simply click the green **Call** button. Because you are chatting with someone, Skype assumes that this is who you want to call. To call someone else, minimize the chat window, and follow the regular procedures for making a call.

## Bookmark a Chat (Create a Persistent Chat)

Skype offers a feature called *bookmarked chat* or *persistent chat,* which is a multiperson chat about a particular topic. A persistent chat may go on for days, weeks, or even months.

Persistent chat is useful for things like focus groups, research teams, and coordinating committees whose members need to communicate small amounts of information quickly over a long period of time.

To start a persistent chat, follow these steps:

1. Invite some contacts to a chat.

2. Click the **Topic** icon on the toolbar above the chat window (see Figure 5-33).

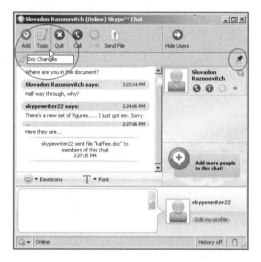

**Figure 5–33** Persistent chat

3. Type a chat topic, and click the **Pushpin** icon (see Figure 5-33).

4. When your mouse pointer is over the pushpin after you clicked it, you will see the words "This chat is bookmarked."

To locate the chat (after you log off and log back on again), choose **Tools** > **Bookmarked Chats** to select the chat. You will see the backlog of messages sent when you were offline. If you do not see any backlogged messages, send an IM to the persistent chat to notify it of your presence. To remove a persistent chat, simply click the blue **Pushpin** icon to unset it.

## Start a Chat from a Recent Chat

In situations where you realize that you have one more thing to add to a chat that you've already completed, you can start a new chat with the same people by using the Recent Chats feature. Choose **Tools** > **Recent Chats** (Mac users: Choose **Chat** > **Recent Chats**), and click the name of the chat you want to rejoin. A new chat window will open, with all the previous participants and chat content.

## View and Clear Chat History

By default, Skype maintains a history of your chats. Chat histories are stored locally on your computer (not in the Skype network) by individual Skype Name. Currently, multiperson chats are not saved in any fashion.

To see the text history of your chats with a specific Skype user, right-click the Skype Name, and select **View Chat History** from the context menu, as shown in Figure 5-34. (Mac users: Control-click the Skype Name, and select **View Chat History** from the context menu.)

**Figure 5–34**   View chat history

To see where the history file is stored on your computer, refer to Appendix B.

To clear your chat history and set your history preferences, choose **Tools** > **Options** > **Privacy**. (Mac users: Choose **Skype** > **Preferences** > **Chat**.) Specify your preferences, and click **Clear History** to delete all history and close any open chats.

NOTE      Chat histories are stored on the computers that were used for the chat. This means that if you have a chat using your computer at work and then come home and resume your chat using your computer at home, both computers will contain a portion of the chat, and neither computer will have the whole history of the conversation.

# File Transfers

Transferring a file using Skype is similar to making a call or starting a chat with Skype. This section covers how to send a file to an individual, to a group, and to all participants of a multiperson chat, and how to accept or deny file transfers.

## Send a File to an Individual

You can send files of up to 2GB to your contacts, but each recipient must have authorized you to see his contact details (you must be able to see his online status), and each recipient must be online to accept the file at the time you want to send it.

If you need to request that someone resend her details, right-click the Skype Name, and select **Request Contact Details** from the context menu. (Mac users: Control-click the Skype Name, and select **Request Authorization** from the context menu.)

To send a file to an individual, follow these steps:

1. Click the recipient's Skype Name.

2. Click the **Send File** icon in the Skype main window.

3. Select a file on your computer, and click **Open**.

   The recipient must accept the file transfer before it can begin.

Alternatively, you can transfer a file by dragging it directly onto a Skype Name. Or you can right-click a Skype Name, and select **Send File** from the context menu. (Mac users: Control-click the Skype Name, and select **Send File** from the context menu.)

In some rare instances, a Skype user may appear online but will not be notified of a pending file transfer until she receives contact from you. If this happens, send a quick IM or call the recipient to reestablish the recipient's connection to the Skype network.

NOTE     File-transfer speed is affected by a number of things. If you are on a Skype call, Skype will prioritize the voice traffic over the file-transfer traffic so that your conversation is not disrupted. Ending your Skype call should improve file-transfer speed.

File-transfer speed can also be affected if your computer is running other programs using bandwidth (such as e-mail or a Web browser) and if not much bandwidth is available from the sender's or recipient's Internet connection. Skype users behind firewalls or Network Address Translation (NAT) devices may also experience slower file-transfer speeds. This is because Skype limits the file-transfer speed to 0.5Kbs for connections that are not routed directly from one computer to another. See Appendix A for more details about how information is transmitted on the Skype network.

## Send a File to a Group

You can also send a file to a group of contacts. Again, each recipient must have authorized you to see his contact details (you must be able to see his online status), and each recipient must be online to accept the file at the time you want to send it.

To send a file to a group of people, follow these steps:

1. Select multiple Skype Names from your Contacts List by holding down the Ctrl key and clicking each Skype Name.

   (Mac users: Hold down the Command key and click each Skype Name.)

2. Click the **Send File** icon in the Skype main window.

3. Select a file on your computer, and click **Open**.

   The recipient must accept the file transfer before it can begin.

## Send a File to All Participants in a Multiperson Chat

To send a file to everyone in a multiperson chat, follow these steps:

1. In the chat window of a multiperson chat, click the **>>** icon at the top of the window, and then click the **Send File to All** icon (see Figure 5-35).

2. Select a file on your computer, and click **Open**.

**Figure 5–35**    Send file to all

## Accept or Deny a File Transfer

Skype is designed so that only people whom you have authorized can transfer files to you. This means that only people to whom you have given access to your online status and contact details can send you files.

Skype does not scan files for viruses, so you should always take precautions when opening files from other parties, just like you do with files sent through e-mail or downloaded from the Web. As a general rule, you should scan all new files with current antivirus software—even files from people you know.

When someone wants to send you a file using Skype, you will see the Receiving File window, shown in Figure 5-36.

To accept the file transfer, follow these steps:

1. Click **Save As**.

   You will see the Enabling File Transfer window.

2. Read the virus warning, and click **Yes**.

3. Select a location for the file, and click **Save**.

4. To open the file immediately, click **Open**; otherwise, click **Cancel**.

**Figure 5–36** Receiving file

To deny the file transfer, follow these steps:

1. Click **Cancel**.

   You will see a message asking, "Are you sure?"

2. Click **Yes**.

   The file will not be transferred to your computer.

In this chapter, you learn
how Skype is used to:

Create new communities

•

Extend business relationships

•

Reach new educational audiences

•

Connect with people in remote places

•

Stay in touch during emergencies

•

Meet people from other countries

•

Develop new hobbies and skills

•

Keep families connected over long
distances (and short ones, too)

# How People Use Skype

## Online Communities

Many Web sites and blogs are devoted to Skype users. The most popular online forums and community sites include

- **Share Skype**—http://share.skype.com. Official Skype blog; includes tools, facts, figures, and other interesting information for consumers and developers.

- **Skype Forums**—http://forum.skype.com. Official Skype Forums covering many topics, including announcements, support, general discussion, suggestions, stories, hardware, payments and billing, SkypeOut, SkypeIn, and voicemail; includes forums for finding people who are willing to be Skyped, as well as a place for hardware and software vendors to post new products and services.

- **Skype Journal**—www.skypejournal.com. Premier independent site for news, views, and support for voice applications, including tips and tricks, product information, and software; for consumers and developers.

- **SomeoneNew**—www.someonenew.com. Meeting site where Skype users can find romance and new friends or simply connect with people with the same interests around the world.

- **The Fooz**—www.thefooz.com. International Internet broadcasting site where Skype users can call in to an ongoing radio program or meet people with the same interests.

- **PSkype**—www.pskype.com. Meeting site where Skype users can find other people who listen to punk, emo, hardcore, indie, Oi!, and ska music.

- **Summit Circle**—www.summitcircle.com. News and expert commentary on Skype and related topics.

- **Internetvisitation**—http://skypetips.internetvisitation.org. Tips, tricks, and best practices for using Skype.

WARNING    When you interact with any group of people online, it is important to be careful about what information you share. Most people on the Internet have good intentions, but you should always be cautious about with whom you share private or financial information, especially in situations with people you don't know very well.

# Skype Stories

The following sections contain stories that highlight how people use Skype to enable business, education, and personal relationships from Montana to Mozambique.

NOTE    The stories here are fictionalized, but they were inspired by real reports of how people are using Skype.

## Extend Business Relationships

Skype allows teams of people in different geographies and time zones to work collaboratively.

### Support Virtual Teams

People who work together but don't reside in the same building (or city, state, or country) use Skype to hold spontaneous meetings.

> I am a manager at a software company that has contract employees in India and Japan. Communication among our staff used to be difficult to coordinate and very expensive. We had one phone meeting that cost $1,200. Now we use Skype to keep "the lines" open, and we can just talk while we work.

### Leave Late-Night Messages

Skype's voice messaging allows users to leave a voice message without having to ring Skype. This feature works much like a text message, but listeners can hear the message with the intent and tones of the caller's voice.

> My team works on different schedules, and I like to work late. At 3 a.m., I can leave a voice message of what I want done for the following day. I don't have to ring anybody's phone or be forced to have a conversation when I just want to leave a message. Voice messages work much better for me than e-mail. Somehow, when my staff hears my voice, we have fewer misunderstandings.

### Reach Clients in Different Time Zones

The online-status indicator allows Skype users in different time zones to know when someone is online and might be available to communicate.

Typically, Skype users in business situations send an instant message (IM) first to find out whether the other person is available to talk.

*I work in Beijing. I have clients who can't keep track of the time difference but don't want to interrupt me during the night. I let them know they can always check my Skype status any time of day. If they see that I'm online, they can just IM me with something like "Are you available for a 2-minute call?" With Skype, they get their answers quickly, without having to wait for an e-mail.*

## Do Business at 35,000 Feet

Airlines like Lufthansa, Japan Airlines, SAS, ANA, and Singapore Airlines now offer Wi-Fi service on their international flights. Korean Air, El Al, China, and Asiana airlines expect to have Wi-Fi within the coming year.

With a Wi-Fi connection, business travelers on long flights can hold Skype meetings, have conference calls, send documents back and forth, and IM colleagues and friends back home. Wi-Fi is significantly cheaper than in-flight phone connections, which cost $8 to $12 per minute.

*I spoke this afternoon with my CEO, who was high over the Atlantic flying home from Eastern Europe. He paid $20 for a Wi-Fi connection for the duration of the flight. The sound quality was as good as ever, and he was just using the built-in microphone on his Mac.*

## Host International Conferences

Skype enables conference calls with up to five people on the same call.

*We recently held our first international panel discussion with university delegates from Sao Paulo, Milan, Dusseldorf, and Cairo. We also had 13 delegates "in attendance" from several universities in the United States via Skype. We set up three laptops with computer speakers and omnidirectional microphones. Each voice came through loudly and clearly, and no one had to strain to hear.*

## Take Meeting Minutes

"Skypecasting" has become a way to share meeting minutes.

*When we have an important Skype conference call, I record the meeting, convert it to an MP3 file, and then send it to my co-workers. For meetings such as requirements sessions, we get an authentic record of what the client actually said.*

## Reach New Educational Audiences

Skype connects teachers with learners even when they are thousands of miles apart.

## Extend Classrooms

When a Skype call is amplified using computer speakers, the volume of a call can be adjusted to fit the size of the room.

*I teach high school students throughout the world how to use software like Photoshop and Dreamweaver via Webconference. I use a Webconferencing tool to provide the visuals. I used to use a speakerphone for the audio, but the speakerphone connection was unreliable, and students often had trouble hearing me. With Skype, students get high-quality sound from their computer speakers, whether I'm teaching a small group or presenting to an audience of 200 kids. And if they need to hear better, they can just turn up the speaker volume.*

## Teach and Mentor

Skype is being used to coordinate long-distance learning.

*I have teachers in local schools in 17 U.S. states. When I'm mentoring a new group, I send out a PowerPoint presentation to each teacher, and we go through it page by page as a group while using Skype to talk through issues and questions.*

## Build Student Communities

Skype is linking long-distance learners.

*We teach online audio engineering courses to students all over the country. Because our students are often isolated from one another, we have implemented Skype to help build a better sense of community. One student in Topeka, Kansas, can interact with another student in Buffalo, New York, who can give advice to a yet another student in Madison, Wisconsin.*

## Connect with People in Remote Places

Skype allows people to talk from places that used to require special communications gear.

### On an island

*I have been visiting a tiny island in the Caribbean regularly for many years now. Until a decade ago, the only connection to the world was a two-way radio. Cell phone service arrived recently, but most island natives can't afford the $4- to $5-per-minute rates. Curiously, the island has broadband Internet access, so I brought Skype to their attention. Island natives can talk freely to their relatives on the mainland for the first time in history.*

### On a mountaintop

*Skype solved the latest of the many challenges I have had getting voice to and from the Sherpas on the slopes of Mount Everest in Nepal. My most recent conversation—at 13,000 feet in Namche, Nepal—was an hour long, clear as a bell, and as loud as when I was up there in person a year ago.*

### In the middle of the ocean

*I work for a telecommunication company in Asia. We provide TCP/IP connections via satellite to ships and shipping companies for low-bandwidth communication (such as e-mail). We decided to test Skype via our shared 64KB global satellite link. Apart from the slight delay that comes with some satellite–earth relay stations, it worked perfectly and was absolutely clear. I was outside in my yard talking to people in the middle of the ocean 1,000 miles away.*

### In a tropical rainforest

*I am writing this by candlelight. The nearest town from here is 3 hours away in the dry season and 3 days away in the wet. I have been working here for a week, and my "officemates" have included monkeys, crocodiles, piranhas, and venomous snakes. There is no telephone here; there is no running water; there is no main electricity. But surprisingly, there is broadband Internet access. My host set it up using a satellite dish, a series of solar panels, and a current inverter. He is an avid Skype user, and just yesterday he talked with the veterinarians at the Jacksonville Zoo.*

### In a war zone

*I'm a director for an international news bureau. Three weeks ago, we were interviewing a reporter in Iraq but were unable to establish a connection via our usual comm links (VPN, satphone, landline, and mobile). I had the reporter initiate a SkypeOut call to us, and it worked really well. The sound was usable, so we aired it to hundreds of radio stations in the United States and millions of listeners nationwide.*

## Stay in Touch During Emergencies

Skype provides an alternative way to stay in touch when communicating is difficult or dangerous.

## Locate Family and Friends

Skype has helped families locate their loved ones when the traditional telephone systems are bogged down and don't work.

*I live in Auckland, New Zealand. My parents, brother, and sister all live in London. The minute I saw the London bombing footage on TV, I desperately tried to reach my parents to find out whether they were all right. I just kept getting the busy signal or the ever-frustrating "Please try again later."*

*I hooked up my headphones, and in seconds, I was talking to my dad with Skype. I tried my brother and sister, and reached my brother at work. He had just spoken with my sister. Everyone was fine.*

## Bypass Congested Networks

Having a SkypeIn number in another country also helps bypass congested networks.

> I was in Paris at the time of the London bombings, but I have clients in Finland who didn't know I was away from the office. They tried my office number in London but couldn't get through. Luckily, I also have a SkypeIn number (in Finland), so they were able to call it and reach me right away.

## Communicate During Wartime

Skype is being used for communications in war-torn areas where making traditional calls can be dangerous.

> My father is overseas as a member of the UN peacekeeping organization. The situation is very tense. He says it is dangerous to use the phone, but yesterday we spoke for nearly two hours using Skype. I feel better knowing what is really going on there (not just what I see on TV), and I felt safer knowing that our conversation was secure and couldn't be tapped.

## Meet People from Other Countries

Skype makes it easy to reach out and talk to new people. The SkypeMe feature connects strangers from across the globe.

> I like to set my online status to SkypeMe just to see who might contact me. Two months ago, I got a call from a retired engineer in Sydney, Australia, who was planning a summer cruise with his wife through Alaska's Passage region. He wanted to know everything from how much American money he should carry to what the weather would be to what side trips he had to take. Now I know who to call when I'm ready to travel to Australia.

SkypeMe connections can also lead to discoveries that cross geographic boundaries and generational barriers. The following was excerpted with permission from John Perry Barlow's online journal BarlowsFriendz:

> I was sitting at my desk in New York on Wednesday night, when Skype started to emit the old-fashioned bell tone that signals a request for a call. The name of the caller was "Kitty." There was also a text chat box on the screen, also from Kitty which read, "I need a friend." I was skeptical. I figured that "Kitty," or whomever, was probably looking for "friends" to come see her "relax" in her Web cam equipped "bedroom." But I took the call.
>
> A delicate Asian-sounding voice came from someplace in cyberspace. "Will you talk to me?" she said. "Why?" "I want to practice my English." "Why me?" "Because your name is John. I think that anybody named John speaks English." I remained skeptical, but further conversation convinced me that she was telling the truth. Kitty turned out to be a 22-year-old girl from Hanoi, who, like her father, works for the state-owned oil company. She had

managed to get five of her neighbors in the Hanoi suburb where she lives to go in on a DSL line and WiFi which she had set up herself. Her boyfriend is off in Korea getting a master's degree in telecommunications. She has three sisters and sent me a picture of her family.

We talked for a long time, in voice, text, photographs, and URLs. I sent her to my home page, so that she could find out more about me. Then I helped her set up an account on Tribe.net, so that people could find out more about her. She sent me a picture of her boyfriend and talked about the dreams they had together. Her spoken English did indeed need practice, but she wrote English with correct lucidity.

We talked a lot about politics and economics in Vietnam. She said she made the equivalent of about 100 dollars a month, that her family was very poor but middle-class by Vietnamese standards, and that they love each other so much that they feel very lucky anyway. Her father had been in the army, making me think that, had things gone a different way, I might have been put in a position to kill him, thus eliminating the possibility of this conversation. I reflected that there are some who visit this blog who even now would think me cowardly and unpatriotic for having refused to be put in that position.

Toward the end of this conversation, I got another invitation to converse. This time, the initiator was "Christine." I answered in text, while continuing my conversation with "Kitty." As soon as Kitty and I signed off, I "rang" "Christine." She was, believe it or not, also a twenty-two year-old from Asia who wanted to practice English. My suspicion that this might be some kind of a scam had dissipated somewhat. Still, I began to think my name might be on some list of easily-distracted English speakers, possibly with a penchant for young Asian women, but they both swore to me that there was no such list and that they had parachuted onto my desktop entirely at random. I believe them. They both seem utterly without guile, and they gave every evidence of being genuinely surprised at what their random troll through Skype's waters had fetched up.

Christine is a business student in university in Shenzhen, Guangdong Province, just north of Hong Kong. Christine speaks extraordinarily clear English, though her writing needs some practice. We went through the same rapid process of getting to know each other. She told me that she dreams to go to Harvard Business School, which she thought was a long shot for someone from a provincial Chinese university. It didn't seem so ridiculous to me. She is obviously very smart and possesses a subtle understanding of the economic epoch in which she and others like her will ascend into global predominance. She was delighted to hear that she'd happened on someone who might actually be able to help her realize this ambition. Lord knows she sounds qualified.

We also had a wonderful dialogue in several simultaneous media. This included an experiment to test Chinese filtration. I sent her to check on a number of Web sites that I thought might be banned in China. None of them were. Nor did she sound like someone who was glancing over her shoulder. She had her own point of view, and she wasn't afraid to state it.

*Now, of course, I know what you're thinking. "Poor old fool doesn't even know when he's being exploited by beautiful young Asian women." If they'd been hunting for rich saviors, they could easily have found better candidates than me. (Listening to Kitty rhapsodize about her boyfriend, of whom she also sent me a picture, makes it very clear that she's not looking for a husband.) Also, neither of them particularly needs saving.*

*The bottom line is this: both of these people reached out at random into the Datacloud and found a real friend. And I feel like I have been graced with a real friend in both of them. Given the fact that I've been getting interesting messages from distant strangers since 1985, why do I think this is a big deal? Why is this different?*

*Because these strangers have voices. There's a lot more emotional bandwidth in the human voice. I'm always surprised by the real version of someone I've only encountered in ASCII. I'm rarely surprised by someone I've only met on the phone. But one doesn't get random phone calls from Vietnam or China, or at least one never could before. Skype changes all that. Now anybody can talk to anybody, anywhere. At zero cost. This changes everything. When we can talk, really talk, to one another, we can connect at the heart.*

## Develop New Hobbies and Skills

Skype creates new ways to collaborate with other people.

## Learn a Language

SkypeMe allows language learners to find native tutors.

*I've already found a couple of new friends to help me practice my Japanese by using the SkypeMe feature with the Japan/Japanese options. I've been studying Japanese for only a year, so when there is a word I don't understand, my tutor friend will just IM the word to me and then I'll look it up.*

## Make Music Online

Skype is helping artists and musicians collaborate.

*I am a beat boxer. I make music and rhythms with my mouth. I've had trouble meeting other beat boxers because I live in a small town in Germany, and the nearest big city is too far for my parents to drive. With Skype, I can meet and jam with beat boxers for hours and never have to leave my room.*

## Play Online

Online gamers use Skype to do "table talk."

*I play online backgammon. I love being able to play whenever I want, but there is something missing when I can't talk to my opponent. I started a Yahoo! group so gamers can get together with Skype. It's made playing online much more action-packed.*

## Rehearse

Actors and comedians rehearse remotely on Skype.

*I had a scene for class I had to rehearse with two other people. I didn't want to miss a weekend getaway with my family just to run lines, so I set up a conference call on Skype. It worked perfectly, and we were able to rehearse the scene many times. I was at the farm with my husband; one woman was on a cell phone at a restaurant in Hollywood; and the other was on a cell phone at the beach, watching her kids.*

## Share Music

Friends far away share their favorite local bands.

*I had my laptop with me at the pub when I suddenly realized that Crazy Cow was getting ready to perform. I immediately Skyped my friend in Taiwan, cranked up the mic, and enjoyed the whole live concert with her. We had a 16-hour difference between us, and she was literally at the other end of the world, but we enjoyed the music together—live—with commentary and a little IM too.*

## Find Love

People use Skype to find love, but even with Skype, love can be tricky.

*I met a woman online who lives in Nevada. We traded e-mails for a while and then I asked her to try Skype. She didn't have a headset at first, so initially, our "conversations" consisted of me talking with her text-messaging me back! Then she got a headset, and we talked for hours at a time. After a month, we decided to meet. I flew to Las Vegas, and in person . . . let's just say that she must have sent me some very old photos. There was no chemistry at all. What a disappointment. Next time, I'm using video calling.*

## Keep Families Connected over Long Distances (and Short Ones, Too)

Skype helps keep long-distance relationships vibrant and alive.

## Share the Small Stuff

Skype allows people to share the sounds of a new place.

*I bought a SkypeIn number in the United States for my sister, and now she calls me frequently. We mainly talk about the small things that happen every day. Yesterday, I sat in a rickshaw with my cellular data connection and allowed her to listen in on the street sounds of Bangalore. It's amazing how the thousands of miles between us can just vanish.*

## Date Long-Distance
Skype helps people who are separated by geography stay close.

> My boyfriend and I used to live 3,000 miles apart. We used to e-mail each
> other every day, but neither of us could afford the phone. Then I heard that
> Skype would work with my university's firewall, so I tried it. We started
> Skyping all the time. We would Skype each other when we woke up, Skype to
> help each other with homework during the day, and Skype to say good night
> each night before going to bed. That was a year ago. We decided to move in
> together, so now I use Skype to call my family.

## Stop Yelling
Getting through to teenagers is also easier with Skype.

> My son is fond of playing on his computer. His room is in the far end of the
> house, and he can't hear me when I'm in the kitchen. I don't like yelling
> (especially when he doesn't answer), so I downloaded Skype onto his
> computer. Now I just call or send an IM when I need to let him know it's time
> to set the table.

## Cook Traditional Family Recipes
Food tastes better.

> My wife uses Skype to make desserts. For baklava:
>
> Ingredients:
> 1 pound phyllo pastry
> 1 cup melted butter
> 2 cups finely chopped walnuts or blanched almonds
>
> For the syrup:
> 1/2 cup sugar
> 1/2 teaspoon ground cinnamon
> 3/4 cup honey
> 1 cup water
> 1 tablespoon lemon juice
>
> Directions:
> 1.  Spread pastry out in a pan.
> 2.  Open Skype on the laptop in the kitchen.
> 3.  Call grandmother in Athens to ask what comes next.

## Help Grandpa Hear

Skype calls received through a pair of computer speakers help older relatives hear.

> *My hearing is not very good. Even at the loudest setting, most phones don't amplify enough for me. With Skype, I can turn up the volume on my computer speakers and hear everything my grandkids have to say! Plus they think it's pretty neat that their grandad knows how to use a computer.*

Skype is being used in variety of ways to improve daily communication and bring the world closer together. New Skype features are being added continually, so the ways people use Skype will continue to expand.

In this chapter, you learn
what to do when you are:

Unable to connect to the
Skype network

•

Experiencing echoes, call
failures, and SkypeOut problems

•

Having trouble hearing (or
others can't hear you)

•

Experiencing other problems,
such as slow file transfers
or CPU overload

# Troubleshooting

This chapter covers procedures, techniques, and workarounds for dealing with the most common problems related to Skype and its operation. The chapter is for both Skype end users and system administrators (or IT personnel) who are still having problems with Skype after reading Chapter 3.

NOTE    For the most current and up-to-date troubleshooting information, refer to the Skype Help site at http://support.skype.com for links to the online knowledge base, interactive troubleshooter, user guides, and Skype Forums (http://forum.skype.com).

## Unable to Connect to the Skype Network: Error 1101, 1102, or 1103

When the Skype application is unable to connect to the network, you will get error code 1101, 1102, or 1103, or the Skype application will continue to display "Connecting" in an ongoing attempt to reach the Internet.

This can happen for several reasons. At home, this typically happens as the result of how a software firewall or router is configured. At work or school, this typically happens as the result of how a hardware firewall or proxy server is configured. In both cases, it can happen as the result of how Microsoft Windows' Data Execution Prevention (DEP) is configured.

### Trouble Connecting at Home

If you're having trouble connecting to the Skype network at home, the first thing to do is determine whether you have a live connection to the Internet. To do this, try checking your e-mail or pointing your Web browser to a Web page that you know changes frequently, such as Yahoo! or Google News.

If you have a connection to the Internet, next determine whether a software firewall is interfering with Skype's ability to connect. To do this, quit Skype, and reconfigure the software firewall as described in Appendix C.

If the problem doesn't appear to be a software firewall, and you are using a router or wireless access point, try restarting or rebooting your router. To reboot a router, follow these steps:

1. Shut down any computer that is connected directly to the router with a wire.

2. On your router, turn the power off or unplug it.

3. Turn *off* your broadband (cable or DSL) modem, and wait 30 seconds.

4. Turn *on* your broadband (cable or DSL) modem, and wait 2 minutes.

5. Turn on the router.

6. Restart the computer.

If you don't have a router, and you are still having problems, log on to http://forum.skype.com, and search for assistance. You can also check the online troubleshooter and user guides at http://support.skype.com.

As a last resort, you can submit a support request outlining the steps you've taken to solve the problem thus far. Be sure to provide a detailed description of your computer configuration, including hardware, operating system, and a list of the programs you are running while trying to use Skype.

## Trouble Connecting at Work or School

If you're having trouble connecting to the Skype network from work or school, contact your system administrator to get help or find out whether Skype is allowed on the network. Some system administrators block peer-to-peer (P2P) programs like Skype to prevent file sharing. If your system administrator has questions about proper network configuration for Skype, refer him to the configuration instructions in Appendix C.

## Microsoft Windows DEP

Microsoft Windows XP (Service Pack 2) and Windows 2000 Server have a configuration option that prevents unauthorized application programs from running. If DEP is enabled and is not configured to allow Skype to run, Skype will crash if you try to start the application.

To reconfigure DEP to allow Skype to run, follow these steps:

1. Choose Start > Control Panel > System.

2. In the System Properties window, navigate to the Advanced tab.

3. In the Performance section, click the Settings button.

   This will open the Performance Options dialog box.

4. Navigate to the Data Execution Prevention tab, and click the radio button labeled Turn on DEP for All Programs and Services Except Those I Select.

5. Click the Add button.

6. Add `Skype.exe` to the list of the programs that DEP will allow.

7. Click Apply and then click OK.

# Echo and Sound-Quality Problems

You may experience echoes, jitters, warbling, and other call artifacts if your computer is old, your Internet connection is slow, or your computer is limited by a highly restrictive firewall. If you are using state-of-the-art equipment, the most common cause of echoes is feedback from one or more parties on a call using a microphone and speakers (instead of a headset).

If you are experiencing echoes, and someone on the call is using a microphone and speakers, try the following:

- Switch to a headset or handset.
- Turn down the volume on the speakers.
- Move the microphone away from the speakers.

For laptops that have fixed locations for their built-in microphones and speakers, the best approach is to get a headset, a USB handset, an external microphone, or a Webcam with a built-in microphone.

If none of these solutions solves the echo problem, try one of the following actions (described in the following sections):

- Turn on Skype's echo-cancellation feature (Mac OS X, Linux, or Pocket PC only).
- Reduce computer bandwidth consumption.
- Disable the capture channel on the sound card (or chip).

## Turn Echo Cancellation On

The echo-cancellation preference for Mac OS X, Linux, and Pocket PC optimizes sound quality through enhanced digital signal processing to reduce the effects of audible echoes on a call. For Microsoft Windows, this feature is permanently configured on and is not available as an option.

Echo cancellation is important in situations where you are using a built-in microphone and speakers; the sound from a speaker can re-enter the microphone and cause echoes. In general, this does not happen when you are using earphones, because the sound between the speaker and the microphone is separated adequately. If Echo Cancellation is off, turn it on.

## Reduce Bandwidth Consumption

The other potential cause of echoes is excessive bandwidth-intensive activity on your computer. If you are engaged in activities that consume large amounts of bandwidth—such as browsing the Web, downloading files, or making Skype calls while streaming media—you may be contributing to the problem inadvertently. Stop these activities one by one to determine which of them is causing the problem.

## Disable the Capture Channel on the Sound Card (or Chip)

Some sound cards and chips have a Capture channel set by default. To avoid hearing echoes on your calls, you may need to go to your sound settings and disable this Capture channel.

# Trouble Making Calls or Processing Payments

Skype displays any number of error codes and error messages if and when there is a problem making a call or processing a payment. These messages typically are not very user friendly; neither are they consistent across operating systems.

## Skype Call Failure: Error 6503, 6504, 10500, or 10503

If you receive error code 6503, 6504, 10500, or 10503 when making a call, it is because the Skype network is temporarily overloaded. Wait a minute, and dial again.

## SkypeOut Call Failure: Error 1040x or 1050x

If you receive error 10404 or 10504 (Mac users: 1040 or 1050) when making calls, it probably is because the SkypeOut number you dialed was not valid or you did not follow the international format for dialing numbers.

The correct format for SkypeOut is + *country code area code number.*

Here is an example:

+16505551212

The country code is 1; the area code is 650; and the number is 5551212.

Check to make sure that you have sufficient SkypeOut credit, and visit the Skype Support site (http://support.skype.com) to get help and information on paid services, payments, and billing.

## SkypeOut Account Suspension: Error 9403, 9407, or 9408

If you receive error 9403, 9407, or 9408 (or other error codes beginning with 940) when making a SkypeOut call, it probably is because a credit-card transaction has been flagged automatically for antifraud verification. This does not mean that anyone thinks you are a criminal, but it does mean that your Skype account has been suspended temporarily from making SkypeOut calls.

To help Skype Technologies resolve this problem quickly, go to the Skype Customer Support site (http://support.skype.com), and submit a support request. To do this, follow these steps:

1. Go to http://support.skype.com/?_a=tickets&_m=submit.

2. In the Department field, select Error 9403 or Error 9407.

3. Type a message.

4. It is strongly advised that you provide the following information:

    - Skype Name

    - Full name

    - Primary contact e-mail

    - First four and last four digits of the credit card used to make your SkypeOut purchase

    - Name of cardholder as printed on the credit card

    - Issuing country of credit card

    If this information is not accessible, or if you used an alternative payment method, you can send detailed information about the payment.

5. Click Submit.

# You Can't Hear

If you can log into Skype but you can't hear sound, you get an error message, or you find that the volume is too soft, you can take a series of actions.

If you can't hear sound at all, or you get an error message, follow these steps:

1. Check the sound output device.

2. Make sure that your headset, speakers, and/or phone device are properly connected.

   The most common problems are issues with physical connections. If you are using a headset, make sure that the speaker plug is plugged into the speaker jack. If you are using powered speakers, the speakers must be plugged in and turned on, and the volume must be turned up.

3. Determine whether your headset, speakers, or phone device is working by playing music files or a DVD.

4. Check the sound output volume.

   Make sure that the sound output is not muted and that the volume is turned high enough for you to hear something.

If you get error code 6101 (Skype cannot find a sound output device that is set up properly on your computer) follow these steps:

1. Make sure that your computer has audio hardware or a sound card.

   Audio hardware is standard in most new computers.

2. Make sure that you have the most recent software drivers for your sound card or sound output device.

   If, for example, you have a USB phone that requires special software drivers, be sure that you have the latest drivers installed. Hardware manufacturers usually make this software available for downloading on their Web sites.

3. Disable any software program that might have taken control of your sound card.

   Software programs such as Total Recorder, Replay Audio Recorder, MP3 Dancer, and Windows XP Voice Recognition can interfere with Skype's operation.

4. Check to make sure that the audio input device you are using is selected as the preferred audio input device.

Refer to the "Sound Setup" section in Appendix C for detailed instructions.

If you can't hear well, follow these steps:

1. Make sure that the volume is turned up high enough on the computer.

2. If you are using speakers or a headset with a volume control, make sure that the volume is turned up.

If these problems persist in Microsoft Windows XP, follow these steps:

1. Go to the Properties window for the specific device.

2. Activate every control.

3. Make sure that each audio level is set properly.

# Others Can't Hear You

If you call the **echo123** answering service and can't hear your own voice on the playback, or if other Skype users report that they can't hear you, follow the steps in the following sections.

## Microsoft Windows

1. Follow the detailed instructions for verifying your sound setup in Appendix C.

2. If you are using an external microphone, make sure that it is connected properly to your computer.

   Specifically, make sure that the microphone and headphone plugs are connected to the correct sockets.

3. Verify that your microphone is working properly.

   If your microphone does not appear to be working, check to see that the sound device is not muted and that the volume is turned up high enough.

   If everything seems to be working on your PC, but you still do not hear your own voice, try this:

4. Choose Start > Programs > Accessories > Entertainment.

5. Click Sound Recorder.

6. When the Sound Recorder panel is displayed, try to record your speech through the microphone you use.

7. Try to play your recording back.

8. If you still can't hear your recording, go the Sounds and Audio section of the Control Panel, and adjust the microphone settings until the recording test works.

   Alternatively, you can try this instead:

   • Choose Start > Programs > Entertainment > Accessories.

   • Select Volume Control.

   • From the Options drop-down menu, select Properties.

   • Make sure that the Mixer Device setting specifies the correct sound card or the microphone you want to use.

   • In the Adjust Volume For list, click the Recording button; make sure that the Microphone checkbox is checked; and click OK.

   • If more than one device is listed, make sure that the microphone is selected and that the microphone volume is greater than 50 percent.

   • If you see a button labeled Advanced, click it. Or, from the Options drop-down menu, select Advanced Controls and then click Advanced.

   • If there is a check in the Microphone Boost checkbox, uncheck it; click Close; and then try calling the **echo123** answering service again. Alternatively, if there is no check, try checking the checkbox; clicking Close; and then calling the **echo123** answering service.

9. If none of these approaches solves the problem, close all application programs other than Skype, and call the **echo123** answering service again.

10. If that doesn't work, reboot your computer, launch Skype, and call the **echo123** answering service again.

11. Adjust the operating system's sound configuration:

   • Choose Start > Programs > Accessories > Entertainment > Volume Control, or right-click the speaker icon in the Windows system tray and choose Volume Control from the context menu.

   • In the Volume Control window, choose Options > Properties, click the Microphone radio button, and click OK.

- Choose Volume Control > Options > Advanced Properties.

- An Advanced button should be displayed below the microphone slider. Click it.

- If you see an option to boost the microphone (Mic Boost), click it and then click Close.

- Set the microphone volume manually to a minimum of 50 percent.

- Ignore the fact that the microphone appears to be muted, because this option is controlled by the Skype application.

12. If you still having trouble, make sure that you have the most recent drivers for your sound card or sound output device.

   Hardware manufacturers usually make this software available for downloading on their Web sites.

13. If you are still having trouble, or you are getting error message 6101 or 6102, it's possible that another application has hijacked the sound card.

   Software programs such as Total Recorder, Replay Audio Recorder, MP3 Dancer, and Windows XP Voice Recognition can interfere with Skype's operation.

14. Shut down any applications that may be using your computer's sound system.

   Try turning all of them off and then turning them back on one by one to determine which one may be in conflict with Skype. See the Skype Forums for more information.

15. If you still are having trouble, try refreshing the connection settings (for advanced users only):

- Close the Skype application.

- Delete the file `shared.xml`, which will be rebuilt automatically when you run the Skype application next. (To find this file on a Windows PC, you need to change your folder options to Show Hidden Files. Then navigate to `C:\Documents and Settings\All Users\Application Data\Skype`.)

- Run Skype, and log in.

16. If that doesn't work, another thing you can do is edit the Skype configuration files (for advanced users only):

- Close the Skype application.

- Navigate to `C:\Documents and Settings\`*`username`*`\` `Application Data\Skype\`*`skypename`*`\`. (To find Skype configuration files on a Windows PC, you need to change your folder options to Show Hidden Files.)

- Replace *`username`* with the Windows login name of the user running Skype, and replace *`skypename`* with the Skype login name of the user running Skype.

- Use a text editor to edit `config.xml`.

- Look for the XML entities `<Call>` and `<General>`.

- If the entries are missing, go to the Skype Forum at http://support.skype.com for guidance. If you see them, try changing the values from 1 to 0, or vice versa. Change the two entries simultaneously. In other words, if they are both 1, change them both to 0.

```
<Call>
<AGC> 1 </AGC>
<General>
<AGC> 1 </AGC>
```

- Run Skype, and log in.

17. If the problem persists, edit `config.xml` again, and look for the XML entity for the microphone volume. `<MicVolume>`.

    If `<AGC>` is set to 0, you can increase the number associated with the microphone volume to a maximum of 255:

    ```
    <MicVolume> 255 </MicVolume>
    ```

## Mac OS X

1. Follow the detailed instructions for verifying your sound setup in Appendix C.

2. If you are using an external microphone, make sure that it is connected properly to your computer.

    Specifically, make sure that the microphone and headphone plugs are connected to the correct sockets.

3. Verify that your microphone is working properly.

    If your microphone does not appear to be working, check to see that the sound device is not muted and that the volume is turned up high enough.

If everything seems to be working on your Mac, but you still do not hear your own voice, try this:

4. Choose Apple > System Preferences > Sound.

5. Make sure that the appropriate microphone is selected, and see whether the input level changes when you speak into the microphone.

6. If you do not see the appropriate microphone, headset, or handset displayed, try disconnecting and reconnecting it.

7. If you are still having trouble, try adjusting the Skype automatic volume settings.

   To do this, go to the sound-devices preference, and disable automating by *unchecking* the Enable Automating Sound Device Settings checkbox.

8. Adjust the operating system's sound configuration:

   • Choose Apple > System Preferences > Sound.

   • Select Input.

   • Adjust the Input Volume slider to a minimum of 50 percent.

   • Talk into the microphone to see how well the sound input level is being registered. If the sound registers to a level less than 50 percent, increase the input volume.

9. If you still having trouble, make sure that you have the most recent drivers for your sound card or sound output device.

   Hardware manufacturers usually make this software available for downloading on their Web sites.

10. If you are still having trouble, or you are getting error message 6101 or 6102, it's possible that another Mac OS X audio application has hijacked the sound card.

    If you are running Virtual PC, software programs such as Total Recorder, Replay Audio Recorder, MP3 Dancer, and Windows XP Voice Recognition can interfere with Skype's operation as well.

11. Shut down any applications that may be using your computer's sound system.

    Try turning all of them on and then turning them back on one by one to determine which one may be in conflict with Skype. See the Skype Forums for more information.

12. If you still are having trouble, try refreshing the connection settings (for advanced users only):

   - Close the Skype application.

   - Delete the file `shared.xml`, which will be rebuilt automatically when you run the Skype application next.

       The most straightforward way to find and delete this file is from the Terminal window. Navigate to `/Users/`*username*`/Library/Application Support/Skype` (replace *username* with the Mac OS X login name of the user running Skype), and delete the file.

   - Run Skype and log in.

13. If that doesn't work, refer to the Skype Forums for the most recent troubleshooting information.

14. Close the Skype application.

# Other Problems

If you are experiencing issues with interactive voice response (or voice-mail) menus, slow file transfers, computer CPU overload, or calls that are dropped repeatedly, this section should help you resolve these types of issues.

## Skype Dial Buttons and Interactive Voice Menu Problems

The Skype dial buttons do not work reliably with all interactive voice response (IVR) systems. If you experience problems using Skype with an IVR system, try being extra careful when you click any button in the Skype dial pad. Otherwise, go to the Skype Forums for hints, tips, and more information.

## File-Transfer Problems

File transfers can be slow for several reasons:

   - **Bandwidth issues**—Either the sender or the receiver does not have a lot of bandwidth, or the bandwidth available is being used by other programs.

   - **Skype call prioritization**—If you are engaged in a Skype call, Skype will prioritize the voice traffic over the file-transfer traffic so that your conversation is not disrupted. The file-transfer speed will improve when you end your Skype call. If you are running other programs that use your bandwidth (e-mail, Web browser, and so on), these will affect transfer speed as well.

- **Files being transferred through a relay host**—Skype limits file-transfer speed to 5 Kbps during relayed transfers. See Appendix A for more information on relay hosts.

## How to Avoid Relayed Transfers (Advanced Users Only)

Skype uses relay hosts to transfer files when two Skype applications cannot communicate directly over the Internet. Often, relayed transfers are caused unnecessarily by firewalls, Network Address Translation (NAT) devices, or routers that are not configured to allow UDP packets out and their replies back in.

Most firewalls, NAT devices, and routers are P2P-friendly, which means that they are configured by default to allow for UDP (user datagram protocol) Consistent Translation. If your network hardware uses UDP Consistent Translation, it means that it is P2P-friendly and will permit high-speed (nonrelayed) Skype file transfers.

As a result, opening ports usually is not required, but in some cases, it can help speed file transfers. Depending on the specific network hardware you have, you may be able to avoid relayed file transfers by ensuring that your firewall, NAT device, or router allows UDP packets out and their replies back in.

Refer to the technical documentation (or the vendor Web site) for your firewall or NAT device to determine whether your router uses UDP Consistent Translation or to learn how to configure your firewall and NAT to allow UDP replies in. Refer to Appendix C for more information.

NOTE    Skype allows system administrators to disable the file-transfer capability. If the Skype application user interface for transferring files is grayed out, it means that someone has configured your Skype application to prevent you from sending or receiving files in this fashion. Refer to Appendix B or consult your system administrator for clarification or help.

## CPU Overload

If you notice your computer acting sluggish or feeling hot to the touch, or you notice the battery draining quickly, Skype may be using too much of your CPU's processing power inadvertently because of a conflict with another application that is running.

This occasionally happens when sound software, such as Total Recorder, is installed and set up as the default I/O device for Skype.

To remedy CPU overload, try one or more of the following solutions:

1. Change the I/O devices for your sound card or USB handset in the Skype preferences, or change the default Windows I/O device in the Windows Control Panel.

2. Lower Skype's task priority (advanced users only):
   - Press Ctrl+Alt+Delete to open Task Manager.
   - Navigate to the Processes tab.
   - Right-click Skype.exe, choose Set Priority from the context menu, and then lower Skype's task-priority level.

## Router Hardware Issues

The most infrequent cause of dropped calls, poor sound quality, and other Skype problems is your network router. That said, it is possible that your router is the root cause of certain problems that are difficult to diagnose and troubleshoot.

Although most routers work well with Skype, certain routers do not. People have reported problems using the following routers with Skype: D-Link 604 nonwireless, D-Link 614 wireless, and Linksys BEFSX41 non-wireless. There may be others as well. Check the Skype Forums and Knowledgebase for the most up-to-date information on hardware that does not work well with Skype.

If you are using a router that people have reported works poorly with Skype, or if you suspect that the problems you are having are related directly to your network hardware, the best alternative is to try a different router.

If you are using a router that should be compatible with Skype, and you suspect that the problems you are having are related to your network hardware, try resetting your router, upgrading router firmware, or reconfiguring your router to allow PC-to-phone communication. Refer to the technical documentation (or the vendor Web site) for your network hardware.

# Skype Architecture

This appendix describes the high-level architecture underlying Skype. It explains the relationship between the Skype software application and its supernode-based peer-to-peer (P2P) network, and it includes a brief history of P2P networks.

This appendix is for people who are interested in the technical aspects and history underlying Skype's architecture. You do not need to read this appendix to use Skype effectively.

In this appendix, you learn how:

- P2P networks function
- P2P networks have grown and evolved
- The Skype application and network function
- Skype routes network traffic using supernodes

## A Brief History of P2P Networks

When you hear people talking about a P2P network, generally, they are referring to two things:

- The format or communications *protocol* that a group of technical people have agreed will be used to transmit and receive data among a particular set of devices that need to share information in a network
- The decentralized P2P computing infrastructure described briefly in Chapter 1

Although not everybody agrees on the exact definition of a P2P network, there is broad agreement that P2P networks take advantage of the processing power, bandwidth, and file-storage and -retrieval capabilities provided by the individual computers in the network (versus using centralized computing equipment and servers). For an illustration of centralized computing equipment and servers, see Figure A-1.

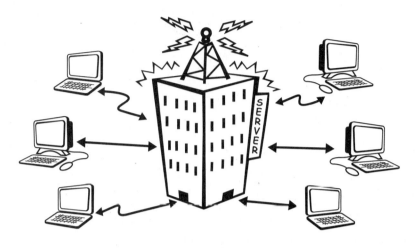

**Figure A–1** Centralized computing equipment and server

In a "true" P2P network, the individual computers and computing devices, or *nodes*, at the edges of the network join dynamically to route network traffic and to process CPU-intensive and bandwidth-intensive tasks (see Figure A-2).

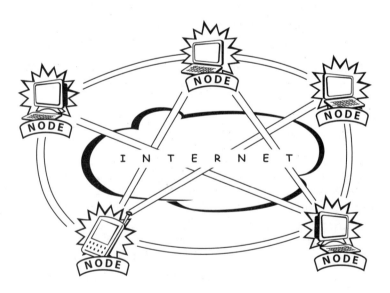

**Figure A–2** P2P decentralized network

The P2P network protocol itself is a technical description of a specific set of rules, as well as the types of interactions or behaviors that result when the rules are enacted. The protocol establishes what the network can do and the capabilities it has to offer. P2P networks also rely on an *application,* which generally is a software program that enables people to use the P2P network for a particular purpose.

You can think of the protocol and application in terms of transportation infrastructure and automobiles. The traffic laws, painted guidelines, signs, and stoplights act like a protocol. They define where vehicles should go and how they should behave. Your car is like an application, because it enables you to accomplish something. If you want to go somewhere, you use the application (the car) and follow the protocols (the rules of the road). The network is the whole system of roads that takes you from place to place.

Different kinds of transportation require different types of vehicles. Different uses of the P2P used to require different types of applications. People exploited applications like the original Napster to swap MP3 files over the Internet, and using the Internet to make voice calls requires an application like Skype.

## The Earliest P2P Networks and Applications

The earliest P2P networks were, put kindly, difficult to use. People didn't think of them as P2P systems per se, because they were limited-use research and business-oriented networks. The early P2P networks were difficult to use because the engineers who designed them were less focused on ease of use and more focused on the technical details related to how the bits of data should be distributed and shared among the peer computers for optimal performance.

Moreover, in the absence of a "killer app" to fuel adoption (such as downloading MP3s), the engineers were less concerned with figuring out how to make the networks simple to search and straightforward to use. Since these early beginnings, three generations of P2P networks have followed.

## First-Generation P2P Networks and Applications

ICQ and to a lesser extent Napster were largely considered to be the first generation of popular P2P networks. These P2P networks worked by allowing someone to connect directly across the network to someone who was using a copy of the same program.

Although there are stronger similarities between ICQ and Skype, Napster provides a simple and straightforward example of how this type of P2P network functioned. Napster (the company) maintained central servers, which hosted a directory search index of the files that each Napster user had on his or her computer. When a user wanted to find a particular MP3 file, he simply searched the network by querying the central directory (see Figure A-3). If the directory search index contained the name of the file the user was looking for, Napster efficiently connected the two nodes directly so that the user could download the song (see Figure A-4).

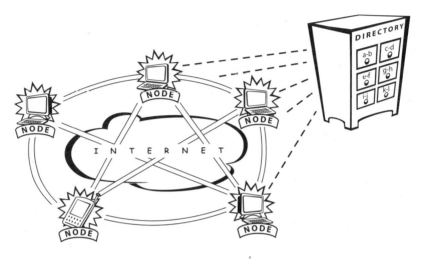

**Figure A–3**   P2P network with a centralized directory

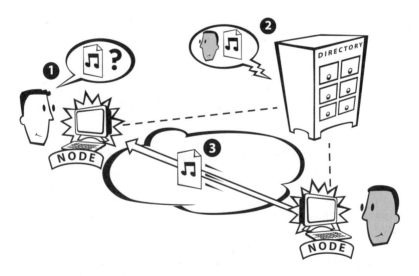

**Figure A–4**   Connecting two nodes directly in a P2P network

The centralized directory turned out to be the Achilles heel of Napster, because it made it easy for lawyers to demand that the service be shut down in response to claims that the network enabled copyright infringement. To shut the network down, the central servers simply needed to be disconnected from the network or unplugged.

## Second-Generation P2P Networks and Applications

The next attempt to create a P2P network was spearheaded at Nullsoft, which was a subsidiary of America Online (AOL). Gnutella was both a remarkably simple P2P file-sharing protocol and an experimental application that avoided the use of a vulnerable centralized directory search index.

Gnutella worked by connecting a given application to a certain number of nodes, which in turn were connected to other nodes, and so on. The decentralized directory was spread across the network to individual nodes and did not rely on any central servers (see Figure A-5).

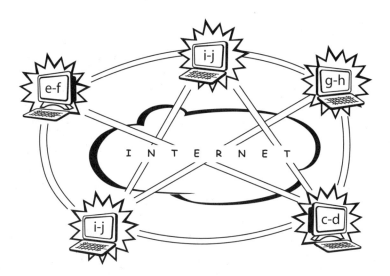

**Figure A–5**   P2P network with no centralized directory

Although this second-generation P2P network did not suffer from the same vulnerabilities as Napster, the design of the protocol was not at all efficient. Searches were slow, and groups of nodes tended to create disconnected islands of subnetworks that couldn't be searched.

Each time a user wanted to search for a file in the network, the user's application had to broadcast the request to the nodes to which it was connected. These nodes in turn had to propagate the request again, and so on until the file was located, if at all.

Gnutella was released briefly in March 2000. Incidentally, this was the same moment that AOL was merging with Time Warner Music and Napster was being investigated. When it became apparent to AOL that Gnutella was theoretically capable of the same types of potential copyright infringement that Napster was being investigated for, it requested that Nullsoft prevent people from downloading it any further.

But the cat was out of the bag. Scores of people had already downloaded the Gnutella application in the short period of time it was available. Soon thereafter, hackers reverse-engineered the Gnutella application, and as a result, the protocol is now in the public domain. Even so, scalability and performance issues have prevented the broad adoption of the Gnutella P2P network.

## Third-Generation P2P Networks and Applications

With Gnutella having paved the road for a decentralized approach to managing the directory search index, the FastTrack protocol emerged as the subsequent generation of P2P technology. FastTrack worked with several well-known applications, the most famous being KaZaA.

The third generation of P2P networks were more evolved because they supported supernodes, which offered significant enhancements over the previous two generations of P2P networks (see Figure A-6). Supernodes allowed for improved search performance, reduced file-transfer latency, network scalability, and the ability to resume interrupted downloads and simultaneously download segments of one file from multiple peers.

A *supernode* is an ordinary node that, under particular circumstances, can take on special tasks. Supernodes improve network scalability by helping nearby nodes join dynamically. Supernodes detect which applications are online, establish connections among them, and guide encrypted traffic efficiently.

Supernodes also work in concert to support a new type of decentralized directory called a *global index* (see Figure A-7). Unlike the second generation of P2P networks, the global index is managed by a hierarchical arrangement of all available supernodes and is not hosted on central servers. When a more powerful computer with a fast Internet connection runs the application software, it may automatically "wake up" as a supernode to act as a temporary directory index server for nearby applications, based on available memory, bandwidth, and uptime.

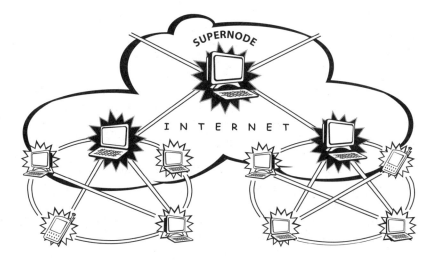

**Figure A–6**   Series of network clusters joined by supernodes

**Figure A–7**   Global index

Like second-generation P2P networks, third-generation networks don't run the risk of being shut down from a central location. Supernodes also enable third-generation P2P applications to work behind most firewalls and Network Address Translation (NAT) devices. So long as two applications can establish an outgoing connection to the Internet, they can communicate regardless of whether they can connect directly with each other.

# Skype Client Application and Network

Skype has two major pieces of anatomy: the application and the network. The Skype application is primarily a communications application, but it also has other key capabilities that integrate voice calling, instant messaging, person-to-person videoconferencing, and file transfers into one seamless program. And there are more capabilities to come. Skype is working on new features, and third-party developers are using Skype's application programming interface to create auxiliary services such as Pamela, which is a programmable answering machine.

On computers, the Skype application works on most popular operating systems. On mobile devices, Skype currently supports devices running Pocket PC. Skype also supports an application for embedded Linux, and Skype Technologies is working on applications for a host of other operating systems, including Symbian.

The Skype application is tightly coupled to the underlying network and relies on an authentication server to ensure that Skype Technologies can retain control of the network. Unlike previous FastTrack applications, the Skype application does not contain any adware, malware, or spyware.

The Skype application looks and behaves slightly differently depending on the device it is on. This is because each device places constraints on the application as a result of its design. On a residential dual-mode phone, for example, screen real estate and file storage are limited, so the application presents a Skype Contacts List but not the ability to transfer files.

The reason why Skype voice quality is so high and speech sounds more natural is that Skype does not have to compress its signal as much as the traditional telephone network does. Connections are also set up directly between peers and don't have to go through a central server, allowing Skype to take advantage of the full available bandwidth of a broadband connection.

Skype uses several voice *codecs* (compression/decompression algorithms) that have a broader frequency range than the 2.4kHz range provided by the traditional telephone network. To compress and decompress speech depending on the available bandwidth, Skype uses enhanced versions of the G.729, G.711, and iSAC codecs, as well as iLBC, which was designed specifically for Internet telephony applications so that sound quality can degrade gracefully when individual data packets get lost.

Skype Technologies is continuing to focus on ease of use, and with each subsequent release, the Skype application is becoming a more full-featured user interface for the underlying network.

## Intelligent Routing with Supernodes

When you download and install the Skype application, your computer becomes part of the Skype P2P network, which is composed of ordinary nodes, supernodes, and relay hosts. Although supernode and relay-host capabilities are built into every Skype application, only a relatively small percentage of nodes ever become supernodes or relay hosts.

When you install the application, Skype installs software and user interfaces that are visible to the end user. Skype also installs software you cannot see that evaluates the capabilities of your computer and network connection to determine how much assistance your computer can provide to the Skype network if required to do so.

Skype's ability to act as a self-forming distributed network is the result of the interaction among ordinary nodes, supernodes, and relay hosts throughout the network.

Under normal circumstances, the Skype application acts like an ordinary node. When running on a fast computer with a broadband connection, however, it may under certain conditions "wake up" as a supernode or relay host to give the Skype network minor but essential additional capabilities—in other words, capabilities beyond those that end users are aware they need.

## Supernodes and Relay Hosts

When a supernode wakes up, it dynamically forms a starlike pattern or local cluster of up to several hundred peer nodes to help leverage all the available resources on the P2P network. A *relay host* is similar to a supernode but is used for a different purpose:

- **Supernodes** act as temporary directory index servers for nearby nodes in the cluster. They are also responsible for detecting which applications are online, establishing connections between them, and passing signaling messages to guide encrypted traffic efficiently.

- **Relay hosts** act as data-transfer stations to connect Skype applications that for some reason (such as a firewall) cannot connect directly.

A Skype user cannot tell whether his computer is being used as a regular node, a supernode, or a relay host because these additional supernode capabilities are transparent and do not have a noticeable impact on a computer's performance.

Supernodes simply hold the directory entries of up to several hundred Skype users. And although supernodes need to accept a relatively small number of directory queries, they do not carry voice, text, or file-transfer data. Supernodes are restricted from using more than 5 kilobits per second of bandwidth. Relay hosts, however, can carry Skype network traffic, but Skype also has strict bandwidth limits for relay hosts. The computing resources required to support the activities of a supernode or relay host are always small compared with relative processing power, memory, storage space, and available bandwidth on a given computer.

Every Skype application stores a list of supernode network addresses that permit a given node to connect with the network. When a Skype application successfully contacts a working supernode, it gets an updated list of network addresses of currently active supernodes for future use. The Skype application selects an active supernode as its "upstream" link and then uploads search requests and other relevant data to this supernode, which in turn communicates with other supernodes to satisfy any search request. A search request might be an authorization, a voice call, an instant message, or a file-transfer request.

In all cases, the Skype application first attempts to communicate with another Skype application directly. When this is not possible, the active supernode routes the connection and the call traffic through relay hosts. Skype opens multiple standby connection paths and then dynamically selects the one with the optimal bandwidth or lowest latency. Then the application connects to a peer node and transfers data, using Hypertext Transfer Protocol (HTTP). This approach increases call-completion rates and improves overall service quality throughout the entire Skype network.

The way that Skype routes traffic means that it can route encrypted calls intelligently through the most efficient and effective path in the network. Instead of routing calls through a centralized system of switches made of hardware circuits, Skype takes advantage of the way that the Internet segments messages into packets, each of which gets transmitted individually and may follow a unique path to its final destination.

As a simple example of how this works, let's say that you and a friend are on Skype, and your friend wants to talk to you. When your friend initiates a call, the Skype application on your friend's computer broadcasts a request to the network—specifically, to a supernode running on a computer somewhere else. In response to this request, the supernode tells the Skype application on your friend's computer where to reach you, and the call gets connected.

Each time a new user joins the Skype network, another supernode potentially becomes available. And as more Skype users come online, the more supernodes become available to expand the capacity of the network.

## Centralized Global Index User Directory

The earliest version of Skype did not use what is now called the global index. It relied on a completely decentralized directory search index in which the supernodes maintained a distributed search index and each user's Contacts List was stored locally in the Skype application on the user's computer.

Starting with version 1.2 of the application, Skype added a limited centralized directory for managing account names, passwords, and e-mail addresses. Skype also added the decentralized directory service or global index to improve the overall quality of the user experience. The global index is not hosted on central servers; instead, it is managed by a hierarchical arrangement of all available supernodes. As a result, your Contacts List is now stored as part of the global index and is available at any computer when you log in to Skype. This allows you to buy a new computer or move from one computer to another and have access to your Contacts List when you log in.

## Firewall and NAT Traversal

Under most conditions, Skype automatically traverses the vast majority of firewall and NAT boundaries, which are associated with roughly 50 percent of the broadband Internet connections in homes and small businesses. Therefore, the problems that people encounter trying to use SIP (Session Initiation Protocol)-based Internet voice solutions are largely averted by Skype's third-generation P2P network architecture.

Skype applications on publicly routable Internet addresses and applications that are not behind firewalls can provide assistance to nodes that are affected by network address translation. This capability to assist applications behind firewalls and NATs permits applications that otherwise would not be able to communicate to connect, as long as they both can make an outgoing connection to the Internet. The result is that when a Skype user initiates a call, the connection is made, regardless of whether the caller or the person being called is behind a firewall or a NAT boundary.

Some software firewalls will interfere with Skype, however. In such cases, the software firewall must be reconfigured to allow Skype to work. Skype cannot traverse proxy servers or authenticated firewalls.

# Skype Security

This appendix provides a somewhat more technical perspective on the security model that Skype uses to maintain privacy. It assumes that you have read Appendix A, which describes the high-level peer-to-peer (P2P) architecture underlying Skype.

This appendix is for people who are interested in the underlying technical aspects of Skype's security model. You do not need to read this appendix to use Skype effectively.

In this appendix, you learn:

- How Skype's security works
- How a Skype session is established and users are authenticated
- How Skype users are authorized
- How encryption is handled
- Where Skype data is stored
- Where to locate more information on Skype security

## Skype Security Linked to Architecture

Skype's security is integrally linked to its architecture. Because Skype employs supernodes and relay hosts, all voice calls, chat messages, and file transfers are encrypted end to end to ensure privacy. As a result, Skype's network traffic cannot be intercepted and decoded while in transit. Currently, Skype is the only Internet voice application provider that uses strong encryption to protect network traffic.

Although Skype does offer a private communication channel, it also runs on mass-market operating systems, so it does not provide a secure computing platform in the strictest meaning of the definition; neither is it a secure file storage solution.

Skype provides an operational level of security or privacy for Skype users in the context of the security provided by Microsoft Windows, Mac OS X, Pocket PC, Linux, and the other operating systems on which the Skype application runs.

The term *secure computing platform* refers to a computing platform that meets technical criteria about how information is transmitted, received, handled, and stored such that high-value or high-risk transactions can be handled securely. In most instances, these platforms are expensive, specialized hardware incorporating built-in cryptography.

Although Skype does not guarantee complete anonymity or secrecy, it does provide *transport-layer security* (described next in this appendix) to ensure that message content traveling over the Skype network on the Internet cannot be tapped or intercepted (and, as a result, will not end up at unauthorized destinations).

At this printing, there are no regulations governing law enforcement's ability to listen in on computer-to-computer voice calls. There are regulations regarding communications over *traditional* phone networks, however. If law-enforcement officials want to listen to a SkypeIn or SkypeOut call, they can approach the traditional phone network termination providers to request access to calls routed to or from the traditional phone networks.

# Skype Transport-Layer Security

*Transport layer* is a term defined by the Open Systems Interconnection (OSI) standard, which is a reference model that speaks to the end-to-end transfer of data between users and systems in a network. Transport-layer *security* is a concept that speaks to the degree to which network traffic between such systems is protected by some sort of cryptographic model.

Skype's use of supernodes and relay hosts as part of its network architecture creates a requirement for robust transport-layer security, because under certain circumstances, Skype network traffic may travel through computers that are not party to a call, text chat, or file-transfer session.

Transport-layer security is important to consumers who are concerned about privacy. This type of security prevents anybody who may have access to a Skype supernode or relay host from interfering with or capturing any part of a Skype communication, even if they somehow manage to collect or sniff network data packets.

For businesses that are concerned about competitive intelligence gathering, strong security is a basic requirement. Working in concert with Skype's supernode-based P2P architecture, the security model prevents a competitor from installing a computer on the Internet in the path of incoming and outgoing calls for the purpose of eavesdropping.

To understand how Skype's security works, first you must understand how the authentication of a Skype user is validated, how a session is established, and how encryption is handled.

NOTE    For the purpose of clarity, the following discussion will not make any distinction between voice calls, instant messages (IMs), and file transfers. It will simply refer to *caller* and *recipient* to prevent any confusion. Please note that any time you see the word *caller*, it could mean that the Skype user wants to initiate any kind of communication supported by Skype, regardless of whether it is a voice call, IM, or file transfer.

## Skype User Authentication

Skype employs the public-key cryptographic model with signed digital credentials to validate the authenticity of Skype users, as well as to reduce the need for centralized infrastructure.

With public-key/private-key cryptography, one of the keys is made public (meaning that it can be broadly distributed), and the other key remains secret. Although the two keys are related, they are independent. There is no way to use one of the keys to determine the other key, and both are needed to complete the transaction.

When an end user signs in using a valid Skype Name and password, the user's Skype application connects to a centralized server for authentication. When the connection is validated, the user's Skype application receives a signed digital credential from the Skype authentication server. This digital credential is signed using a private key that is maintained at Skype Technologies.

The public key required to verify another user's digital credential is stored in each Skype application and must be used to validate the digital credential. Signed digital credentials are valid for only a certain period and are renewed periodically by Skype Technologies to enhance security further.

When the Skype application receives a signed digital credential and validates its authenticity, that credential can be presented to other Skype applications on behalf of a given user who is trying to establish contact. When the authentication process is complete, there is no need for any recipient to check in with any centralized infrastructure to verify a caller's authenticity.

NOTE    To the Skype network, a Skype user is a simply a Skype Name that has been authenticated properly to the network. Although a Skype user typically runs only one Skype application instance, an individual can have multiple Skype accounts with unique Skype Names, passwords, and profiles.

## How a Session Is Established

When one Skype user wants to communicate with another Skype user, the connection and session are established in a very specific way. A description of this process illuminates where transport-layer security is necessary to ensure privacy on the Skype network.

When a user is online, his Skype application maintains a persistent connection to a supernode. This persistent connection is what allows Skype to provide a useful and consistent sense of a user's presence and availability on the network.

When starting a call, IM, or file transfer, the caller's Skype application first tries to determine whether the recipient is online, using the global index—the distributed database of users that is maintained in the supernodes.

If the recipient is online, the caller's Skype application gets the network address for the recipient's Skype application, as well as the network address for its associated supernode, both of which are stored in the global index.

Then the caller's Skype application attempts to make a direct connection to the recipient's Skype application. If a direct connection is established, the call, IM, or file transfer begins (see Figure B-1).

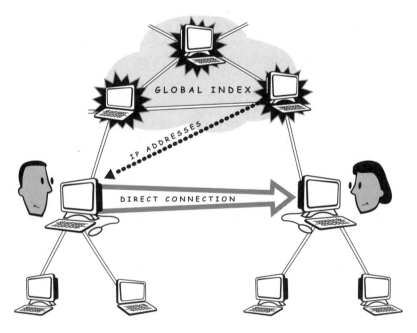

**Figure B-1** Establishing a direct connection

Sometimes, however, a direct connection cannot be established immediately without additional assistance. This often happens when a recipient is behind a firewall or Network Address Translation (NAT) device. When this happens, the caller's Skype application sends a message to the recipient's supernode, requesting that it be forwarded to the recipient's Skype application. The message from the caller's Skype application is intended to alert the recipient's Skype application that there is a desire to connect with it, as well as an inability to make a direct connection.

This message signals the recipient's Skype application to try to make direct contact with the caller's Skype application in the opposite direction. If a connection can be established using this reverse path, the call, text chat, or file transfer begins (see Figure B-2).

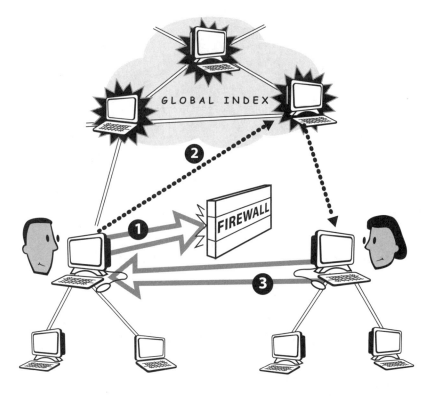

**Figure B–2**  Establishing a reverse connection

If, however, it is impossible for the two Skype applications to communicate directly, the call, IM, or file transfer must be routed through other special nodes on the Skype network, called *relay hosts.*

Next, both the caller's and recipient's Skype applications connect to the relay hosts. When this happens, the conversation is spread among the relay hosts to ensure call quality, completion, and fault tolerance (see Figure B-3). The relay hosts remain active for the duration of the session.

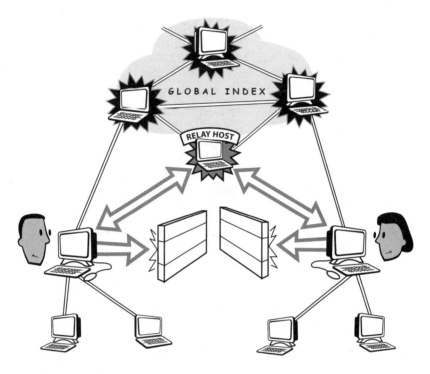

**Figure B-3**    Establishing a connection with relay hosts

Transport-layer security is a fundamental requirement in the Skype P2P architecture, because to complete a connection, supernodes and relay hosts—peer nodes that are not party to the call—may be involved. The Skype security model prevents relay hosts from eavesdropping on relayed calls, because all communication between the caller and recipient is encrypted end to end between pairs of nodes (see Figure B-4).

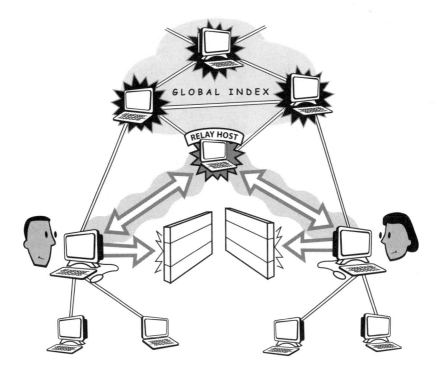

**Figure B–4** End-to-end security

When a connection is established (but before a voice call, text chat, or file transfer begins), each Skype application involved in the session must present a digital credential and agree on an Advanced Encryption Standard (AES) encryption key, which is described in the following section.

## How Encryption Is Handled

Skype relies on a system of public and private keys to keep the contents of communication confidential. All Skype network traffic is encrypted to ensure privacy. This includes all signals used to control the Skype network, as well as communications content, such as voice, text, and data. The use of encryption here means that it is not possible to know what information is traveling in the Skype network among nodes, supernodes, or relay hosts.

The cryptographic model behind Skype employs both public-key and symmetric-key cryptography, including the AES algorithm, used in 256-bit integer counter mode.

NOTE  AES, which was originally named Rijndael (pronounced "Rhinedahl") after its inventors, has been adopted by the U.S. government to protect sensitive information. In 256-bit encryption, a total of 1.1 x 1,077 possible keys are provided to encrypt the data actively in each Skype call, IM, and file transfer.

Skype also uses 1,024-bit RSA to negotiate symmetric AES keys. User public keys are certified by the Skype server at login, using 1,536- or 2,048-bit RSA certificates.

When a connection is established as described earlier in this appendix, each Skype application generates half of a 256-bit symmetric key. These keys are exchanged and joined to create a 256-bit session key, which is valid for the life of the session. Each session gets its own 256-bit key. In the case of a three-party conference call, three simultaneous calls are set up, each with its own session and different key. This sharing of symmetric AES keys makes it possible for Skype to be an authenticated channel between two or more valid Skype users.

For efficiency, Skype relies on public-key cryptography to validate signatures on credentials for the purpose of negotiating a symmetric key; then it uses symmetric-key cryptography for secure communication between Skype applications. The public-key cryptographic model enables a Skype application to receive private messages that only it can read and to issue signed messages that no one else could have created.

No one (not even Skype Technologies) has a copy of the key shared by the parties to a call. There is neither sharing nor disclosure of keys to any parties other than the pairwise sharing to establish a 256-bit session key. And when a session ends, the keys are discarded. Encryption keys are neither escrowed to third parties nor disclosed to the Skype users.

# Security and File Transfers

Skype's file-transfer capability provides a convenient new channel for sharing photographs, documents, and other electronic files among Skype users. Along with this newfound ability, however, comes the risk of inadvertently downloading a file that contains a virus, Trojan horse, spyware, or adware. (For a definition of these terms, see the "Adware and Spyware" section later in this appendix).

You must take special precautions when accepting files—in the same way that you would be careful with opening e-mail attachments, sharing files, or downloading directly from the Internet. Before you use Skype's file-transfer capability, make sure that you have up-to-date antivirus software that is configured to scan all incoming files, even from people you know.

IT managers may have an additional concern. Because Skype network traffic is encrypted, it is important to remember that incoming file transfers are decrypted by the Skype application before they can be scanned. This isn't a problem, however, because the "shield" capabilities provided by all the major antivirus software vendors enable real-time scanning.

As a result, if an antivirus product is running, if the virus definitions are up to date, and if a Skype user receives a virus-laden file via Skype, the shield will stop the file from arriving. Today, however, antivirus products simply close the Skype application and display a warning message, because Skype currently does not support centralized scanning for viruses.

On the Microsoft Windows platform, file transfers can be blocked by setting Registry keys for the computers on which the Skype application is running. See Appendix C for more information on blocking file transfers.

# Skype User Authorizations (Privacy)

The Skype application offers a set of features to give you control of who can see your presence information (online status) and who can contact you.

To protect privacy, Skype has a system called authorizations. A Skype *authorization* is the right that one Skype user grants another Skype user to see her online status. Each time someone adds you to her Contacts List, she must make a request to see your online status information. If you authorize the request, this person will be able to see when you come online or go offline. If you deny or ignore the request, your online status information will not be available to this user.

An authorization is not simply a flag or a bit that gets set somewhere in the message. It is a digital signature assigned to the authorization that is then sent to the requestor, and it is tied to the same sign-in credential that is used to authenticate identity. Therefore, it is nearly impossible to spoof this system into making Skype act as though an authorization has been made when it hasn't.

You can still be on someone's Contacts List without having authorized him to see your online status, just as someone can be on your Contacts List without your having the authorization to see his online status.

Authorizations are important for maintaining privacy, and they are essential for maintaining control of who can contact you. Skype allows you to set your own privacy thresholds for who can call you, send you IMs, and transfer files. You can specify that:

- Anyone can call.
- Only people on your Contacts List can call.
- Only people you have authorized can call.

IM preferences can be set independently of calls, so you can specify that:

- Anyone can IM you.
- Only people on your Contacts List can IM you.
- Only people you have authorized can IM you.

File-transfer preferences can be set independently of both calls and IMs.

NOTE     Although you can't revoke an authorization, you can block a user (which is effectively the same thing). Blocking a user prevents her from communicating with you and seeing your Skype status, even if the user was authorized previously. If you remove a block, the previously issued authorization remains valid.

Refer to "Set Your Skype Preferences" in Chapter 4 for instructions on configuring authorizations.

# Where Sensitive Data Is Stored

Skype maintains information related to you in six places: the Skype central authentication server, Skype account servers, the Skype event server, the global index in the Skype P2P network cloud on the Internet, your computer, and other Skype users' computers.

- **The Skype central authentication server** stores data about all valid Skype users. This database does not accept queries. Specifically, it stores your Skype Name, your e-mail address, and an encrypted representation of your password. This representation is stored, technically speaking, as a one-way encrypted hash of your password for the purposes of allowing you to log in to the network or reset your password, should the need arise.

- **Skype account servers** collect and process statistics about Skype phone calls for the sole purpose of operating the Skype service. Skype-to-Skype traffic data is collected only in the aggregate. Skype Technologies does not track information about which users are communicating with one another over the Skype network or the duration of these interactions. Information about SkypeIn and SkypeOut calls is collected and processed. If you have SkypeOut credit, information about the calls you place is collected to maintain your account balance.

- The **Skype event server** is a database that Skype employs as a cache to store temporarily a copy of certain types of information, such as voicemail messages. If at all possible, Skype does not maintain copies of information. In the event that the intended recipient is not online for an extended period, however, the message is stored in the event server to ensure that it is delivered reliably—that is, when the recipient comes online next, at which time the message is delivered and deleted from the cache.

- The **global index** maintains your computer's last network address, the network address, your Skype application's supernode, and your current Skype user profile. All profile data in the public directory is digitally signed.

- **Your computer** stores the installed version of Skype, any residual copies of Skype installation files that have not been deleted, voice-mail message files (for messages that have already been transferred from the caller's computer), call logs, chat logs, and a file called `config.xml` that (among other things) contains the Skype Names of people in your Contacts List. Note that chat logs are stored as application data as HTML in the format `skypename.html`, where `skypename` is the Skype Name of the Skype user with whom you have chatted. Note that by default, chat logs are saved indefinitely unless you delete them. Chat logs are stored in a hidden directory under the user's home directory. You can configure Skype to delete them, however, or set them to expire after a given period of time. Here are the locations of the folders where Skype stores data:
  - Microsoft Windows—`C:\Documents and Settings\`*username*`\Application Data\Skype`
  - Mac OS X and Linux—`/Users/`*Username*`/Library/Application Support/Skype`

- **Other Skype users' computers** may contain traces of information and conversations they have had with you. In particular, their Contacts Lists might list you as a Skype user, regardless of whether you have given them authorization to communicate with you. If you and the other user have not been logged on to the Skype network at the same time, any unsent voicemail messages may be present on the other user's computer. The other user's Skype call log may reflect that the two of you have communicated or attempted to communicate. And his chat logs may contain pieces of conversations he has had with you.

WARNING    About your Skype password: Skype Technologies never, under any circumstances, requests your Skype account name or password by e-mail. Your Skype password should remain completely secret. The only place your Skype password is ever required is for logging into your Skype account through the Skype application or the Skype Web site. If you want to create a new password, you can go to your account page on the Skype Web site if you provided a valid e-mail address in your Skype profile.

# Adware and Spyware

The Skype application and installation program *do not* include any adware or spyware:

- **Adware** is software that displays advertising. Some types of adware display advertising only when the program you installed alongside it is running. In other cases, adware displays advertisements regardless of whether the application is running. Most end users consider adware to be irritating and visually distracting.

  When adware is installed on your computer, it generally is done without your consent or knowledge. This is a risk of downloading and installing any software from the Internet. In some cases, the end-user license agreement that accompanies the software does, in fact, disclose that adware will be installed alongside the application. These license agreements typically are complex, however, and disclosures generally are buried deep within the agreement or hidden by obscure language.

- **Spyware** is software that "spies" on you for someone else's benefit. Spyware surreptitiously captures and clandestinely reports information on your computing behavior, habits, or interests for fraudulent or commercial exploitation. The most benign spyware secretly reports the Web pages you browse to collect marketing data. More insidious spyware captures e-mail addresses; passwords; financial data; and in some cases, all the keystrokes that an end user types on her computer.

Adware, spyware, and other forms of malicious code have become a serious problem for people who use Microsoft operating systems, such as Windows 2000, Windows XP Home, and Windows XP Professional. To date, Mac OS X and Linux users have not been as likely to run into problems with adware and spyware, in part because these operating systems have not been popular targets and in part because they have historically had stronger security.

For a detailed explanation of how this data is used, refer to "Privacy, Personal Data and Traffic Data" in the Skype Terms of Service, available on the Skype Web site.

# Skype Security Evaluation

The Skype Web site also contains resources for network administrators and more detailed information on Skype security. Go to www.skype.com/security to find specific security guides for advanced users, network administrators, and security personnel.

This link also includes security bulletins and a Skype security evaluation report by Tom Berson of Anagram Laboratories. This report provides

- An in-depth review of the security framework that is incorporated into Skype products
- A description of the protective mechanisms that are in use throughout the Skype infrastructure
- The general security policy that defines the basis for all designs within Skype's operational framework

# Advanced Setup

This appendix covers advanced setup and configuration topics for both Skype end users and network administrators (or IT personnel).

In this appendix, end users learn how to:

- Verify and configure the sound setup
- Configure software firewalls
- Translate the Skype user interface into other languages

In this appendix, network administrators learn how to:

- Verify the authentic of a Skype installer for mass deployment
- Optimize Skype to work on a local-area network
- Respond to questions about antivirus scanning

## End-User System Configuration

Installing Skype usually doesn't require any advanced setup or special configuration. Sometimes, however, advanced setup is necessary to troubleshoot common problems and reconfigure overly restrictive software firewalls so that Skype can function at its full potential.

This section covers adjustments to the audio playback, recording, and audio device settings on your computer, and how to configure the most common software firewalls.

### Sound Setup

In most cases, your computer's default sound settings will work with Skype. You may want to confirm that the settings are correct, however, and change them if they are not.

Before you change your sound settings, it is a good idea to make a test call to the **echo123** answering service to determine whether you need to make any changes. For more details about making a test call, see Chapter 4.

This section covers the sound setup for:

- Microsoft Windows 2000 Windows or Windows XP (classic style)
- Microsoft Windows XP (XP style)

- Mac OS X 10.3 (Panther) or later
- Linux

**NOTE** You may notice slight differences between the instructions here and what you see on your computer, depending on the specific version of your operating system and the specific audio software and hardware you are using.

## Windows 2000 or Windows XP (Classic Style)

To confirm that your sound settings are configured correctly, follow these steps:

1. Open the Sound and Audio Devices Control Panel.

   - Choose Start > Settings > Control Panel.

   - Depending on whether you have Windows 2000 or Windows XP, double-click either Sound and Multimedia or Sounds, Speech and Audio Devices. The Control Panel should appear.

2. Verify or set the playback options.

   - Select the Audio tab to expose Sound Playback, Sound Recording, and MIDI Music Playback.

   - In the Sound Playback section, make sure that the preferred device's drop-down menu displays the sound device that Skype should be using.

   - Click the Volume button (directly below the Sound Playback Default device drop-down menu). The Playback Volume control is displayed.

   - Choose Options > Properties to expose the volume controls.

   - Check any boxes that are unchecked, and click OK. The Volume control is displayed again.

   - Be sure that the Microphone volume controller for playback is muted and that its checkbox is checked.

**NOTE** Other volume controllers *should not* be muted: Mute All and Wave Mute must be not be muted. Make sure that those checkboxes are *not* checked.

   - Choose Options > Exit.

3. Verify or set recording options.

- In the Sound and Audio Devices control panel, select the Audio tab to expose the Sound Playback, Sound Recording, and MIDI Music Playback sections.

- In the Sound Recording section, make sure that the preferred device's drop-down menu displays the sound device that Skype should be using.

- Click the Volume button (directly below the Sound Recording Default device drop-down menu). The Recording control is displayed.

- Choose Options > Properties. The audio Properties panel is displayed.

- Locate the section that shows the volume controls.

- Check any unchecked checkboxes, and click OK. The Recording Control Panel is displayed again.

- Be sure that the Microphone volume controller for playback is muted and that its checkbox is checked.

NOTE    For Skype to work properly, all other options and channels *must not be checked.*

- In the Recording Control Panel, choose Options > Advanced Controls (if it is not already selected) to expose the Advanced Controls button. Click the Advanced button.

- In the Other Controls section, if there is a MIC Boost checkbox, make sure that it is *not* checked; then click the Close button.

- In the Recording Control Panel, choose Options > Exit.

4. Test your Windows Sound Recording software.

- Choose Start > Programs > Accessories > Entertainment.

- Click Sound Recorder. The Sound Recorder application is displayed.

- Attempt to record and play back your speech through the microphone you plan to use with Skype.

- If you are unable to hear your recording, return to Sound and Multi Media or Sounds and Audio Devices, depending on whether you have Windows 2000 or Windows XP. The Control Panel should appear.

- Select the Sounds tab, and increase the Sound Volume. You can also try returning to the Audio tab and playing with the microphone settings until the recording/playback test works as expected.

5. Verify that the Skype configuration uses the correct sound devices.

  - Start Skype.

  - Choose **Tools** > **Options**.

  - Choose **Sound Devices**, and verify that the Windows default device is selected in the **Audio In**, **Audio Out**, and **Ringing** drop-down menus if you are using only one audio device (such as a headset or microphone and speakers)

  - Click **Save**.

If Skype does not work properly after you finish the sound setup, refer to Chapter 7 or visit the Skype online help center at http://support.skype.com.

## Microsoft Windows XP (XP Style)

To confirm that your sound settings are configured correctly, follow these steps:

1. Open the Sound and Audio Devices Control Panel.

  - Choose Start > Control Panel > Sound, Speech, and Audio Devices. The Control Panel is displayed.

  - Locate the Sounds and Audio Devices section.

2. Verify or set the playback options.

  - Select the Audio tab to expose Sound Playback, Sound Recording, and MIDI Music Playback.

- In the Sound Playback section, make sure that the Default Device drop-down menu displays the sound device that Skype should be using.

- Click the Volume button (directly below the Default Device drop-down menu). The Playback Volume control is displayed.

- Choose Options > Properties to expose the volume controls.

- Check any checkboxes that are unchecked, and click OK. The Volume control is displayed again.

- Be sure that the Microphone volume controller for playback is muted and that its checkbox is checked.

NOTE    Other volume controllers *should not* be muted: Mute All and Wave Mute *must not be muted.* Their checkboxes should be *unchecked.*

- Choose Options > Exit.

3. Verify or set recording options.

- In the Sound, Speech, and Audio Devices Control Panel, select the Audio tab to expose the Sound Playback, Sound Recording, and MIDI Music Playback sections.

- In the Sound Recording section, make sure that the Default Device drop-down menu displays the sound device that Skype should be using.

- Click the Volume button (directly below the Default Device drop-down menu). The Recording Volume control is displayed.

- Choose Options > Properties. The Properties panel is displayed.

- Locate the section that shows the volume controls.

- Check any unchecked checkboxes and then click OK. The Recording Control Panel is displayed again.

- Be sure that the Microphone volume controller for playback is muted and that its checkbox is checked.

NOTE    For Skype to work properly, all other options and channels *must not be selected.*

- In the Recording Control Panel, choose Options > Advanced Controls (if it is not already selected) to expose the Advanced Controls button below the Microphone volume controller. Click the Advanced button.

- In the Other Controls section, if there is a MIC Boost checkbox, make sure that it is not checked; then click the Close button.

- In the Recording Control Panel, choose Options > Exit.

4. Test your Windows Audio Recording software.

- Choose Start > Programs > Accessories > Entertainment.

- Click Sound Recorder. The Sound Recorder application is displayed.

- Attempt to record and play back your speech through the microphone you plan to use with Skype.

- If you are unable to hear your recording, return to the Sound, Speech, and Audio Devices Control Panel.

- Select the Sounds tab, and increase the Sound Volume. You can also try returning to the Audio tab and playing with the microphone settings until the recording/playback test works as expected.

5. Verify that the Skype configuration uses the Windows default device.

- Start Skype.

- Choose **Tools** > **Options**.

- Choose **Sound Devices**, and if you are using only one audio device (such as a headset or microphone and speakers), verify that the Windows default device is selected in the **Audio In**, **Audio Out**, and **Ringing** drop-down menus. Optionally, you may elect to have Skype ring the speaker in your PC when a call comes in. To do this, check the **Ring PC Speaker** checkbox. Then, in either case, click the **Save** button.

If Skype does not work properly after you finish the sound setup, refer to Chapter 7 or visit the Skype online help center at http://support.skype.com.

## Mac OS X 10.3 (Panther) or Later

To confirm that your sound settings are configured correctly, follow these steps:

1. Open the Sound Preferences.

   - Choose Apple > System Preferences > Sound. The Sound System Preferences window is displayed.

2. Verify or adjust the output sound preferences.

   - First, make sure the output is not muted. (The Mute checkbox should not be checked.) Optionally, you can configure Mac OS X to show the volume in the menu bar at the top of the screen, which lets you adjust the sound volume directly (that is, without having to open the Sound System Preferences first).

   - In the section that allows you to choose a device for sound output, verify that the device you want to use with Skype is selected; otherwise, select it. Doing this configures Mac OS X to route sound from all applications (including Skype) to this device by default.

   NOTE    Mac OS X presents only sound output devices that are available for immediate use. Therefore, if you want to use a USB headset, you need to plug the headset into the USB port on your Mac before Mac OS X recognizes the device as available for use.

   - The Skype application also allows you to choose a sound output device that is different from the Mac OS X default device. See step 4 for instructions on how to do this.

3. Verify or adjust the input sound preferences.

   - In the section that allows you to choose a device for sound input, verify that the device you want to use with Skype is selected; otherwise, select it. Doing this configures Mac OS X to route sound to all applications (including Skype) to this device by default.

   NOTE    Mac OS X presents only sound input devices that are available for immediate use. Therefore, if you want to use an external microphone, you need to plug the microphone into the appropriate port on your Mac before Mac OS X recognizes the device as available.

- The Skype application also allows you to choose a sound input device that is different from the Mac OS X default device. See step 4 for instructions on how to do this.

- Set the input volume as high as possible without causing any audio distortion.

- When you have selected the sound input device, you can adjust the input volume to send the best audio signal to the Skype application. Set the input volume option in the middle (to 50 percent).

- Speak into your microphone in a normal voice, and watch the input level vary with your voice. For best sound quality, the input level should be greater than 60 percent but not exceed 75 percent. Increase it as much as possible without exceeding the 75 percent threshold.

- Set the output volume at about 75 percent to start. You can change this later easily without having to open Sound Preferences.

- Verify that the Mute checkbox is not checked.

4. Verify or change Skype audio preferences (optional).

- Although Mac OS X gives you a certain amount of control of your sound preferences, Skype allows you to customize further the way sound is managed to give you some additional control.

- Skype allows you to treat "Skype sound" differently from the way that other sound is handled. You can configure Skype to override Mac OS X sound-handling capabilities to use a Bluetooth headset, for example, while Mac OS X still routes music from iTunes through speakers.

- To do this, follow these steps:

- Start the Skype application.

- Choose **Skype** > **Preferences**. The Preferences panel is displayed.

- Select **Audio**.

- In the **Audio Output** and **Input** drop-down menus, select the device(s) you want to use with Skype.

- To reduce the possibility of echoes in your voice calls, check the **Echo Cancellation** checkbox.

- To prevent sound distortion from the overamplification of sound input, check the **Gain Control** checkbox.

5. Test your Skype application software.

If you cannot get Skype to work properly after verifying or changing the Skype audio preferences, make sure that you have set the Sound Playback and Recording preferences properly, as described in steps 2 and 3. Otherwise, refer to Chapter 7 or visit the Skype online help center at http://support.skype.com.

## Linux

Setting up sound on Linux can be tricky because of differences between the older Linux OSS (Open Sound System) and the more modern ALSA (Advanced Linux Sound Architecture), as well as variations in the many Linux distributions and hardware devices.

This section assumes that you have read and are familiar with the Skype installation instructions in Chapter 3. In addition, it assumes that you will type all the operating-system commands described in this section in a terminal window: the console, a GNOME terminal, xterm, or another terminal window.

Moreover, the information on sound setup for Linux is evolving. For the most current and up-to-date tips and tricks, best practices, and other information on using Skype with Linux, visit the Skype Forums at http://forum.skype.com.

NOTE     If you see the message "Sound device is not defined," you can safely ignore it. This message appears when Skype employs the default sound device /dev/dsp, because a particular device was not specified in the Skype sound configuration.

## OSS

Skype provides native support for OSS. For version 2.4 or newer kernels, however, some users report that it is easier to set Skype to work with ALSA drivers and OSS emulation than with a pure OSS kernel. See the "ALSA" section that follows for details.

To use Skype with OSS, follow these steps:

1. Select the DSP (digital signal processing) audio device for your sound card.

   Generally, the audio device name is /dev/dsp, which assumes a device number of zero. If you have more than one sound card, you might want to designate additional audio devices for each card, such as /dev/dsp1 and so on.

Enable microphone input in the audio mixer setting.

2. You can use the aumix, kmix, or gnome-volume applet.

3. Try setting the input capture source to use the microphone.

   If the sound is distorted, and your hardware allows you to turn capture off, turn capture off. Input capture works differently, depending on your operating system and hardware configuration.

4. Make sure that the microphone volume controller is set high enough that your voice will be sufficiently loud.
   You can always change this setting later.

## ALSA

Currently, Skype does not provide native support for ALSA. As described in Chapter 3, however, you can use ALSA devices if you install the ALSA OSS emulation layer, which is effectively the same as running Skype with OSS. If you have ALSA with dmix (kernel stream mixer) enabled, running Skype should be no different from running it with the native OSS. To use Skype with ALSA, follow these steps:

1. If you have not already done so, install the ALSA OSS emulation layer.

2. Make sure that you have the snd-pcm-oss and snd-mixer-oss modules in your kernel.

   They can be compiled in the kernel or loaded separately. Check for these modules by typing the following command as root:

   ```
   # lsmod
   ```

3. If these modules are not already installed, try to load them.

4. As root, type the following:

   ```
   # modprobe snd-pcm-oss
   # modprobe snd-mixer-oss
   ```

If you get an error message when you execute either of the preceding commands, you might need to upgrade your kernel. Before you do that, however, consider consulting a Linux system administrator or searching the Skype for Linux Forum at http://forum.skype.com.

If your computer motherboard has 5.1 sound support, you need to turn off the mixer options Mic As Center/LFE and Line As Surround. Note that these options typically are not present in native OSS. Motherboards with 5.1 support should be used in conjunction with ALSA anyway, however.

## KDE Default: aRts

aRts (Advanced Real-Time Synthesizer) is the default with the KDE desktop. If aRts sound is working, so should Skype. Make sure you run Skype through the `artsdsp` program.

Verify that the `aRts` Full Duplex option in the KDE Control Center is set to *on*. This helps ensure that the microphone will work and that you do not get a segmentation fault that you can avoid.

To do this, follow these steps:

1. Choose Control Center > Sound & Multimedia > Sound System.

2. Select the Hardware tab.

   A Full Duplex option should be displayed.

3. Make sure that the Full Duplex checkbox is checked.

4. Start Skype in the directory where the Skype application is executable:

   ```
   # artsdsp -m ./skype
   ```

5. If you hear an echo, you may try decreasing the `aRts` sound buffer size.

6. Choose Control Center > Sound & Multimedia > Sound System.

7. Select the General tab, and go to the Skip Prevention section.

8. Try decreasing the sound buffer size to less than 200ms.

## GNOME Default: ESD

ESD (Enlightened Sound Daemon) is the default with the GNOME desktop. To run Skype with GNOME, follow these steps:

1. Run the `esd` daemon, using the `-d` flag to specify `/dev/dsp`.

   This is because the `esddsp` wrapper in some Linux distributions (such as Gentoo) checks for the presence of esd daemon parameters, and the daemon will not be detected if these parameters are not present. To do this, type the following:

   ```
   # esddsp -d /dev/dsp
   ```

2. Run Skype through to enable the sound.

3. Start Skype in the directory where the Skype application is executable.

### GStreamer, NMM, and NAS

Currently, there is no way to enable Skype sound through GStreamer. It is recommended that you disable GStreamer and use either the ALSA or OSS method described earlier in this appendix.

In addition, other outdated audio servers, such as NAS (Network Audio Server) and NMM, are also unsupported. Again, disable them, and use either the ALSA or OSS sound system.

### "Hijack" /dev/dsp for Different Playback and Recording Devices

There are times when you might want to use different /dev/dsp devices for recording and playback. You might want to use your microphone with /dev/dsp and use a set of USB speakers on /dev/dsp1, for example.

Currently, Skype does not provide support for this in the Skype application. You can use a tool called Skype DSP Hijacker, however, to accomplish this. The tool, skype_dsp_hijacker, and instructions for using it are available at http://195.38.3.142:6502.

Simply follow the instructions to build and install the appropriate version of the tool. Then run Skype as described in the instructions.

# Software "Personal" Firewalls

A *personal firewall* is a piece of commercial software installed on a computer that is designed to prevent unauthorized and potentially damaging communications from reaching the computer and adversely affecting its operation.

As awareness and concerns about Internet security have increased, so has the adoption of personal firewalls. In fact, the Microsoft XP operating system with Service Pack 2 now includes a software firewall as part of its standard installation. These software firewalls work much like traditional hardware firewalls: They allow only trusted communications to pass through the firewall to the heart of the computer while other, unauthorized communications are blocked.

To work properly, the Skype application must be able to communicate with the Internet. By default, however, a computer with a software firewall will often block communication that is necessary for Skype to work.

This section describes how to configure these industry-standard firewalls:

- Windows Firewall for Windows XP Service Pack 2
- Trend Micro PC-cillin Internet Security
- McAfee Personal Firewall Plus
- Symantec Norton Personal Firewall

- ZoneAlarm Pro
- Mac OS X Firewall

## Windows Firewall for Windows XP Service Pack 2

This section covers configuring the Windows Firewall on an individual PC and for a group.

### Individual PC

To set up the Windows Firewall to work properly with Skype, follow these steps:

1. Open the Windows Firewall Control Panel by choosing Start > Control Panel > Windows Firewall.

2. Select the General tab (if it is not already selected).

3. Determine whether the Windows Firewall is On (Recommended) or Off (Not Recommended) (see Figure C-1).

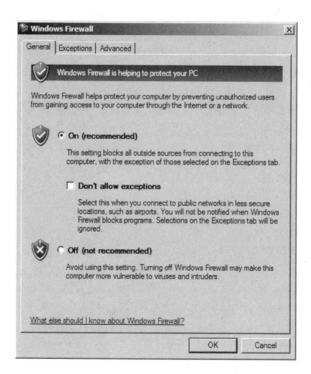

**Figure C–1**  Windows XP Service Pack 2 Firewall on

By default, the Windows Firewall should be On unless a third-party firewall has been installed that has deactivated the Windows Firewall.

If the Windows Firewall is off, close the Windows Firewall Control Panel, and set up the third-party firewall to work with Skype. Otherwise, if no third-party firewall is installed, turn the Windows Firewall on to safeguard the computer from malicious network activity.

4. Assuming that the Windows Firewall is on, make sure that the Don't Allow Exceptions checkbox is *unchecked*. If there is a check in the checkbox, uncheck it.

5. Select the Exceptions tab.

6. If you see Skype in the Programs and Services list, make sure that the Skype checkbox is checked (see Figure C-2), and click OK.

Skype should be listed with a check in the Programs and Services list.

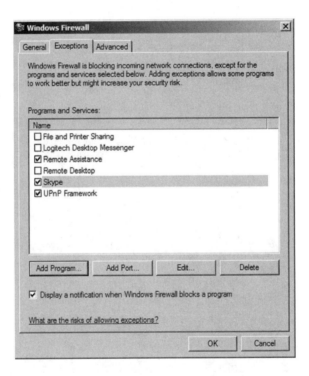

**Figure C–2**   Windows XP Service Pack 2 Firewall exceptions

If you do not see Skype in the Programs and Services list, click Add Program; select Skype from the Programs list; and click OK. Skype should be listed with a check in the Programs and Services list.

7. Click OK to finish.

8. Click OK to confirm any changes you have made.

9. Close the Windows Firewall Control Panel.

Skype should work properly now. If it does not, refer to Chapter 7 or the Skype Forums at http://forums.skype.com for more information on how to get Skype to work properly.

## Group Policy Settings

If you are a system administrator responsible for managing a Group Policy object for a Windows application, you can optimize a network for Skype by applying an exception in the Group Policy snap-in.

To add an exception rule to your existing policy settings, set the Group Policy Setting profile:

```
Computer Configuration/Administrative Templates/Network/
   Network Connections/Windows Firewall/Standard Profile
```

The policy setting should be:

```
Windows Firewall: Define program exceptions (Enabled)
```

Here is the specific program exception definition that you should add:

```
%PROGRAMFILES%\skype\phone\skype.exe:*enabled:Skype
```

## Trend Micro PC-cillin Internet Security

To set up the Trend Micro PC-cillin Internet Security firewall to work properly with Skype, follow these steps:

1. Open the Trend Micro PC-cillin Internet Security firewall, and select the Network Security tab on the left side of the window.

2. Click Personal Firewall.

   The Personal Firewall window is displayed.

3. Determine whether the firewall is on or off.

   The firewall should be on.

   If the firewall is off, and you are using Windows 2000, the firewall is not the cause of the problem. If you are using Windows XP, it's possible that the Windows XP Service Pack 2 Firewall is on.

4. Select the active profile (indicated by the green ball), and click Edit.

   The Personal Firewall Profile window is displayed.

5. Click the Exception List tab.

6. Find Skype in the list of exceptions.

   You should see two entries for Skype: one for incoming connections and another for outgoing connections (see Figure C-3). If you see two entries for Skype, skip to step 10.

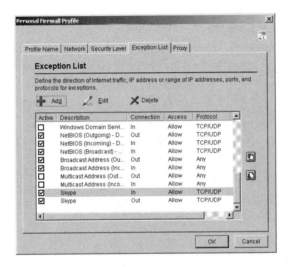

**Figure C–3**   Trend Micro PC-cillin Firewall exceptions

7. If you do not see Skype listed in the Exception List, or if you only see one entry for Skype, click Add.

   The Add/Edit Personal Firewall window is displayed.

8. In the Description field, enter **Skype**; allow *outgoing* TCP and UDP message packets through the firewall on all ports (see Figure C-4); and click OK.

9. Click Add again.

   The Add/Edit Personal Firewall window is displayed.

10. In the Description field, enter **Skype**; allow incoming TCP and UDP message packets through the firewall on all ports (see Figure C-5); and click OK.

If the Permissions column indicates that the permissions for Skype are set to allow access, Skype should be working.

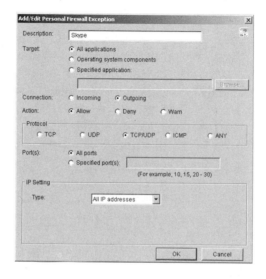

**Figure C–4**   Trend Micro PC-cillin Firewall allowing outgoing messages

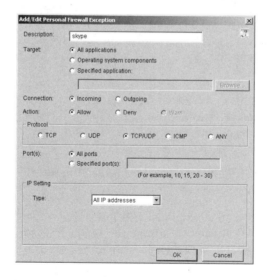

**Figure C–5**   TrendMicro PC-cillin Firewall allowing incoming messages

11. If Skype isn't working, close the Trend Micro PC-cillin Internet Security firewall, and refer to Chapter 7 or the Skype Forums at http://forums.skype.com for more information on how to get Skype to work properly.

   If the Permissions column indicates that Skype is blocked, edit the permissions to allow TCP and UDP messages to get in and out so that Skype can communicate with the Internet properly, and close the Trend Micro PC-cillin Internet Security firewall. Skype should work properly. If it does not, refer to Chapter 7 or the Skype Forums at http://forums.skype.com for more information on how to get Skype to work properly.

## McAfee Personal Firewall Plus

To set up McAfee Personal Firewall Plus to work properly with Skype, follow these steps:

1. Open McAfee Security Center, and select the Personal Firewall Plus tab on the left of the window.

2. Select View the Internet Application List.

   A new window is displayed, showing a list of software applications that access the Internet.

3. Find the column with the Skype application name (see Figure C-6).

   If you do not see Skype listed in the Internet Applications list, click New Allowed Application, create a new exception, and allow full access for Skype. If the Permissions column indicates that the permissions for Skype are set to allow full access, Skype should be working.

4. If Skype isn't working properly, close McAfee Personal Firewall Plus, and refer to Chapter 7 or visit the Skype Forums at http://forums.skype.com for more information on how to get Skype to function properly.

   If the Permissions column indicates that Skype is blocked, change permissions to allow full access so that Skype can communicate with the Internet, and close McAfee Personal Firewall Plus. Skype should work properly. If it does not, refer to Chapter 7 or the Skype Forums at http://forums.skype.com for more information on how to get Skype to work properly.

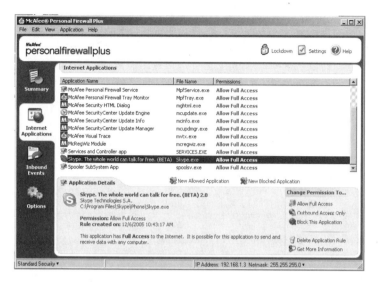

**Figure C–6** McAfee Personal Firewall Plus exceptions

## Symantec Norton Personal Firewall

To set up the Symantec Norton Personal Firewall to work properly with Skype, follow these steps:

1. Open Norton Internet Security; select Norton Personal Firewall; and click Configure.

2. Click Norton Personal Firewall on the left side of the window.

3. Determine whether the firewall is on or off.

   The firewall should be on (see Figure C-7). If the firewall is off, and you are using Windows 2000, the firewall is not the cause of the problem you are experiencing. If you are using Windows XP, it's possible that the Windows XP Service Pack 2 Firewall is set on instead.

4. Select the Programs tab.

5. In the Manual Program Control section, find Skype in the list of programs.

   If the Internet Access column indicates that the permissions for Skype are set to permit all access, Skype should be working. If it isn't, close the Norton Personal Firewall, and refer to Chapter 7 or the Skype Forums at http://forums.skype.com for more information on how to get Skype to work properly.

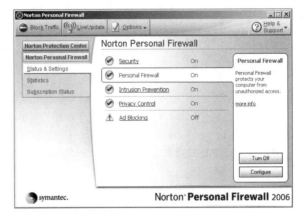

**Figure C–7**    Norton Personal Firewall on

If the Internet Access column indicates that Norton Personal Firewall is set up to block all or provide custom access, continue to the next step to change the permissions so that Skype can communicate with the Internet.

6. Select Skype, and in the Internet Access column, click the drop-down menu to set the access level to Permit All (see Figure C-8).

**Figure C–8**    Norton Personal Firewall manual program control

7. Click OK and close Norton Personal Firewall.

Skype should work properly.

## ZoneAlarm Pro

To set up the ZoneAlarm Pro firewall to work properly with Skype, follow these steps:

1. Open the ZoneAlarm Pro firewall, and select the Program Control tab on the left side of the window.

2. Select the Programs tab (if it wasn't already selected), and find Skype in the list of programs.

3. Find the Skype row.

4. In the Skype row, right-click each question marked ? or X to display a context menu of options (see Figure C-9).

5. Set the Trust Level option to Trusted.

**Figure C-9**   ZoneAlarm Pro trust level

6. Set the options for Access, both Trusted and Internet, to Allow.

7. Set the options for Server, both Trusted and Internet, to Allow.

8. Set the option for Send Mail to Allow (see Figure C-10).

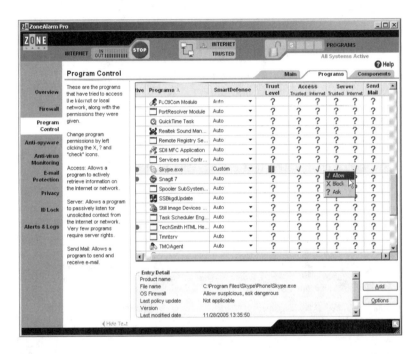

**Figure C-10**   ZoneAlarm Pro Trust Level settings

9. Close the ZoneAlarm Pro firewall.

Skype should work properly. If it does not, refer to Chapter 7 or the Skype Forums at http:// forums.skype.com for more information on how to get Skype to work properly.

## Mac OS X Firewall

Although Skype works properly with the Mac OS X Firewall without any additional configuration, optimizing the Mac OS X Firewall's settings can improve Skype sound quality. To improve Skype performance, follow these steps:

1. Launch Skype.

2. Choose **Skype** > **Preferences**.

3. Select **Advanced**.

4. Write down the port number listed for Connection: Port.

   This number is different for each Skype installation.

5. Open Mac OS X System Preferences; select Sharing; and then choose Firewall.

6. On the right side of the Allow list, select New.

   A drop-down menu is displayed.

7. Click the drop-down menu, and select Other.

8. In the blank space for Port Number, Range or Series, enter the port number you wrote down in step 4.

9. Enter **Skype** for the description.

10. Close the Sharing and Preferences windows.

    Skype should work even better now.

# Run Multiple Instances of Skype

If multiple people are using the same computer under different logins, you can set up multiple instances of Skype. By *multiple instances,* we mean that for each computer login, you can run a copy of the Skype application with a unique Skype Name.

To do this, you must have configured each login and instance of the Skype application to use its own sound devices. Login User1 (as Skype Name "Person1") is configured to use the Headset, for example, and Login User2 (as Skype Name "Person2") is configured to use a USB Handset.

In this situation, however, only one computer login session will be active in the foreground at any time. As a result, multiple people can receive calls using the same computer, but only one login session will contain a Skype application that is able to make outgoing calls from the Skype interface on the computer.

If the handset and sound hardware being used support dialing, however (as is the case with the advanced USB handsets, such as the Linksys CIT200 Cordless Internet Telephony Kit), multiple users can make and receive calls.

# Translate the Skype User Interface into Other Languages

The Skype application was developed in English, but it was designed to allow people to change the language associated with the user interface. Users can choose a language other than English, if the appropriate language definition file has already been loaded into Skype, or translate the application into a language that is not yet available.

To change the Skype application user interfaces into an alternative language, choose **Tools** > **Select Languages** and then select the preferred language.

To translate the Skype application into a language that is not yet available, choose **Tools** > **Edit Skype Languages File**. A language UI Text Editor appears.

In the left comments column, the Skype application user interface item name to be translated is displayed. The middle column displays the original version. The right column displays the translated text, which you can edit.

The name of each item in the left column indicates where in the user interface the item will show up. Items that contain MENU, for example, are Skype application menu items; items that contain CAPTION appear in the title of the Skype application dialog boxes; and items that contain HINT provide information for mouseovers.

Some of the item names in the comments column might not be obvious or self-evident. You can apply your changes and see them displayed in the Skype application immediately, however.

Translating the Skype application user interface involves editing the entire right column into a new language. When you are done editing the language file, click **Save As**, and add the .lang extension to the file name. To make the language translation available in the Skype application, click the **Load** button, and select a file with the .lang extension.

Visit the Skype Forums at http://forums.skype.com for more information on translating Skype and loading user-defined languages.

> Note    The About page does not need to be translated, because the Skype application does not load the legal text on the About page in other languages.

# IT Administration and Network Configuration

Although Skype is used primarily as a consumer application, it is finding its way into organizations of all shapes and sizes. Skype is easy to deploy and install from a central location, and it can be configured to run inside a local-area network, as long as the network allows Skype to communicate with the Internet.

This section covers how to verify the authenticity of the Skype installer and how to configure a network to make it Skype-friendly. It also covers how Skype works with antivirus scanners.

## Verifying Installer Authenticity

To ensure that you have the most current and authentic version of the Skype application, download it from the Skype Web site at www.skype.com/download, and verify the software installer's digital signature.

You may be able to get the Skype application from third parties as well, because Skype Technologies SA allows third parties to host downloaded versions of the application as long as the third party adheres to the terms of Skype's End User License Agreement (EULA) regarding the redistribution of Skype software. In particular, third parties may not repackage or wrap the Skype application in any other software.

NOTE   When the Skype application is installed, it periodically checks to see whether an update is available. The Skype application does not update itself. Instead, by default, it notifies the user that a Skype software update is available, leaving it up to the user to decide whether to upgrade. This automatic update-notification feature is controlled by a Skype application preference setting (choose **Tools** > **Options** > **Advanced**), which you can change if you so desire.

Skype software installers for Microsoft Windows XP, Windows 2000, and Windows Pocket PC 2003, as well as the Skype application itself, are digitally signed. To protect against the installation of malware or spyware, verify the Skype installer's digital signature manually before you run it.

Skype for Linux distributions that are packaged in `rpm` format are signed using Skype's signing key, which you can download from the Skype Web site at www.skype.com/products/skype/linux.

## Microsoft Windows

To verify installer authenticity, follow these steps:

1. Locate the Skype installer program by opening Windows File Explorer and navigating to it.

2. Right-click the Skype installer program, and select Properties from the context menu.

   The Properties dialog box for the Skype installer is displayed.

3. Look for the Digital Signatures tab at the top of the Properties dialog box.

   If you do not see this tab, skip to the "Problems with a Digital Signature" section that follows. If you see the Digital Signatures tab, continue to step 4.

   In the Properties dialog box, a list of digital signatures that apply to this installer is displayed. You should see only one signer of the installer package: Skype Technologies SA.

4. Double-click the line that contains Skype Technologies SA.

   This displays a window that contains the details of Skype's digital signature.

5. Verify that the pop-up window labeled Digital Signature Information indicates that this digital signature is OK.

   If the pop-up window indicates that the digital signature is not valid, stop, because there is a problem, and skip to the "Problems with a Digital Signature" section that follows. Otherwise, continue to step 6.

6. Click the View Certificate button to display the details of the digital certificate that was used to sign the installer software.

   The pop-up window labeled Certificate should present this:

   ```
   issued to: Skype Technologies SA
   Issued by: VeriSign Class 3 Code Signing 2001 CA
   ```

   If the text in either of the fields in the pop-up window is different from what is shown above (except for the year of the signing, which changes each year), stop, because there is a problem with the installer's digital signature. Then skip to the "Problems with a Digital Signature" section that follows. If it is OK, continue to step 7.

7. Click the Details tab to display the serial number of the signing certificate.

8. Verify the certificate serial number with the appropriate serial number, available from the Skype Security Web site at www.skype.com/security.

   If the certificate serial number for your copy of the Skype installer does not match precisely the one you get from the Skype Web site, stop, because there is a problem with the installer's digital signature. If this happens, skip to the "Problems with a Digital Signature" section that follows.

9. If you had no problems with the digital signature verification process, you can safely install the Skype application.

You can perform the digital signature verification test on an installed Skype executable program when the Skype installer has been run, but it is best to verify the authenticity before installing and running the application.

## Problems with a Digital Signature

Invalid digital signatures can appear on downloaded files for several reasons. The installer may have been corrupted accidentally while it was being downloaded, or Skype may have been bundled improperly with a third party's software without Skype Technologies' permission. Alternatively, someone might have violated Skype Technologies' EULA and tampered with the software to incorporate spyware, adware, or malware.

If you discover any problem with a Skype digital signature, it is important that you:

- Do not use or run any copy of the Skype installer that has failed a verification.
- Contact Skype security via e-mail at security@skype.net, and provide the details, including the problem you experienced and where you obtained the Skype installer.
- Download a fresh copy of the Skype installer from the Skype Web site, and verify the authenticity of the new installer as described in the preceding section.

## Skype on a Local-Area Network

The Skype application has certain requirements for network connectivity to work properly and others to enable optimal sound quality. This section describes how to configure a network to be Skype-friendly. This means that the Skype application will be able to connect to the Skype network, and it means that the sound quality will be optimized as well.

Among other aspects of local-area network configuration, this section discusses hardware firewalls. For information on software or "personal" firewalls, refer to the "Software 'Personal' Firewalls" section earlier in this appendix.

First, the Skype application must be able to reach the Internet to connect with the Skype authentication and event servers, as well to connect with other nodes, especially supernodes. This connectivity is required for Skype to function properly.

Second, although Skype will work on most internal networks (behind a hardware firewall), the configuration of the network may have an impact on the quality of the experience for the Skype users who are being served by the local network. Specifically, sound quality may suffer.

This is the result of countermeasures or workarounds that Skype employs automatically to reach the Internet through a less-than-ideal network configuration. The farther the network configuration is from ideal, the more likely that factors such as network speed and latency will adversely affect sound quality.

## Configuring Local-Area Networks and Hardware Firewalls

Network administrators can optimize the Skype user experience by tuning how a network handles the transmission of TCP and UDP packets. They can accomplish this by adjusting the control parameters on networking appliances such as routers, firewalls, and NAT devices:

- Outgoing TCP connections should be allowed to remote ports 1024 and higher, and if possible, outgoing TCP connections should be allowed to remote ports 80 and 443 as well. Skype will *not* work reliably if *all* these ports are blocked.

- Outgoing UDP packets should be allowed to remote ports 1024 and higher. For UDP to be useful to Skype, the NAT must allow for replies to be returned to sent UDP datagrams. (The state of UDP "connections" must be kept for an absolute minimum of 30 seconds; up to an hour is preferred.)

- The NAT translation should provide consistent translation, meaning that outgoing address translation usually is the same for consecutive outgoing UDP packets.

Although the use of UDP is optional, Skype relies heavily on UDP packets to optimize sound quality and speed file transfers through Skype. For UDP communications to work properly for Skype through a NAT device, however, the translation rules for UDP packets must be handled consistently. In other words, UDP packets sent from one external network address and port number must be translated consistently to an internal network address and port number without varying either the network address or the port number. Call quality will be much better, on average, if the caller is able to send UDP packets to the called party and receive UDP packets as answers.

NOTE    Setting incoming ports in firewalls usually is straightforward. Some routers, however, allow you only to configure incoming TCP port forwarding (which you should do) and do not allow you to reconfigure incoming UDP ports.

## Is Your Network Skype-Friendly?

Most routers, firewalls, and NAT devices are Skype-friendly, which means that by default, they are configured to handle UDP traffic properly.

You can accomplish this with a freeware program called NAT Check, written by Bryan Ford, that allows you to test your network to see whether the UDP translation is compatible with peer-to-peer (P2P) protocols such as Skype. You can download NAT Check freeware for Microsoft Windows, Mac OS X, and Linux from http://midcom-p2p.sourceforge.net.

To make sure that UDP traffic is handled properly, be certain that the network's UDP translation shows consistent translation, that the input and output ports are identical except in the event of a conflict loopback translation, and that unsolicited UDP packets sent to the network are filtered or discarded.

Finally, although it's not a requirement, it is preferable for the network's firewall or NAT gateway to support IP packet fragmentation and reassembly. In addition, the firewall must not block an attempt to send parallel UDP packets or TCP connection attempts to multiple ports at the destination address, because some firewalls mistakenly classify this type of behavior as port scanning and, as a result, block the host. This type of behavior would not only have an adverse affect on Skype, but also may have a negative impact on other legitimate network applications running on the same host computer.

## Skype and Proxies

Skype fully supports SOCKS5 and HTTPS/SSL proxies, including optional authentication.

For SOCKS5, the proxy must allow unrestricted TCP connections to at least port 80, port 443, or high-numbered ports (those numbered 1024 and higher). For HTTPS/SSL proxies, the proxy must allow unrestricted TCP connections for port 443. You can optimize proxy settings in the Skype options.

NOTE    On Microsoft Windows platforms, Skype uses the proxy settings in Microsoft Internet Explorer to determine which proxy settings, if any, to use. The Skype user, however, can set the SOCKS5 or HTTPS/SSL proxy manually, including any required user name and password for proxy authentication.

## Antivirus Scanners

Skype introduces the same risk to end users as e-mail or other file-transfer services, provided that an industry-standard antivirus product is installed on the Skype user's computer and that the virus definitions are kept up to date.

In commercial environments, the concern is that because Skype network traffic is encrypted end to end, users might unwittingly accept an infected file through Skype's file-transfer capability, and the file will be decrypted on the user's computer before it can be scanned by antivirus software.

The Skype application is compatible with the "shield" antivirus scanning products from all major antivirus vendors, however. Therefore, although the Skype application itself does not yet include support for integrated, centralized antivirus scanning, it does allow for standard scanning by antivirus products on the sender's and receiver's computers.

Skype employs industry-standard techniques for creating files, as well as for reading from and writing to them. When a program wants to read from or write to a file on disk, the application in question calls the appropriate kernel primitives to attempt the file access. When Skype reads a file, the user begins to transmit, or when the Skype application writes the file on the receiving end of a file transfer, the Skype application makes requests to create, open, and read from or write to the file as appropriate. When an antivirus program is used, the program inserts itself into the file access chain, which allows it to monitor file content constantly for patterns that match known virus signatures.

Antivirus tools exploit the fact that all file access is performed through a small number of kernel primitives by employing one of several techniques to "shim," wrap, or intercept all operating system calls to all file-access kernel functions, depending on the operating system.

Therefore, if a Skype user attempts to send or receive a file, the antivirus program will detect the attempt to read or write a file that contains a virus or Trojan horse and simply deny the Skype application permission to continue writing the file. From the user's perspective, the situation is handled in much the same way that infected e-mail attachments are dealt with; in other words, the file is repaired or quarantined, or the file transfer fails.

Although Skype currently does not provide support for centralized virus scanning, it does allow system administrators to configure Windows Registry keys to disallow all file transfers via Skype.

## Disabling File Transfers in Windows

Refer to the security section of the Skype Web site for more information on how to disable the Skype file-transfer capability in Windows Registry. Go to www.skype.com/security for details.

# Index